Reporting Iraq

AN ORAL HISTORY OF THE WAR BY THE
JOURNALISTS WHO COVERED IT

EDITED BY MIKE HOYT, JOHN PALATTELLA,
AND THE STAFF OF THE *COLUMBIA JOURNALISM REVIEW*

MELVILLE HOUSE PUBLISHING
HOBOKEN, NEW JERSEY

Fallujah, November 13, 2004. AP Wide World/Anja Niedringhaus

© COLUMBIA JOURNALISM REVIEW, 2007

MELVILLE HOUSE PUBLISHING
300 OBSERVER HIGHWAY
THIRD FLOOR
HOBOKEN, NJ 07030

WWW.MHPBOOKS.COM

ISBN: 978-1-933633-34-3

FIRST MELVILLE HOUSE PRINTING: OCTOBER 2007

BOOK DESIGN: BLAIR & HAYES

A CATALOG RECORD FOR THIS BOOK
IS AVAILABLE FROM THE LIBRARY OF
CONGRESS.

ON THE COVER: IRAQI SHIITE MEN CARRY RELIGIOUS
FLAGS ON A PILGRIMAGE TO KARBALA. THE
PILGRIMAGE, BANNED UNDER SADDAM HUSSEIN, HAD
LAST BEEN MADE IN 1977. APRIL 19, 2003.REUTERS/
YANNIS BEHRAKIS/LANDOV

PRINTED IN MEXICO.

Contents

You have to rely on someone who's from there, who's bringing you the tapes, and then you have to piece together what happened from accounts from the military, accounts from eyewitnesses, accounts from hospital figures, all of whom maybe have credibility problems. You have to piece together the best you can to come up with a mosaic of what's going on. That's the reality of it.

—RICHARD ENGEL, APRIL 2006

Up until that moment, my experiences of people dying in front of me came from movies. And then you believe that someone is hit, or losing a leg, they will be screaming like hell. And everyone is silent. Everyone is silent, no one is screaming. Another guy was crying, weeping, an old man, a big fat guy, was weeping silently. And I remember I was so scared and I was trying to lay flat, but still I would try to stand up, take a couple pictures, and then lie back down again....Up until this moment I was separated from the scenes of car bombs by my lens: it was something else, it was not reality because I see it through this viewfinder, and all you care about is the light, where it's coming in, the composition, the light. So you are separated. But the smell, the smell is always there. But that day, when you are part of the scene, when you are hiding, all these kids behind this building, and you are trying to take shelter and you are trying to make yourself flat, and you wish that your height is only two inches so you can go flat to the curb. It was that day when this glass wall that was separating me from the scenes of car bombs shattered.

—GHAITH ABDUL-AHAD, APRIL 2006

Introduction

Not long after President George W. Bush landed on the USS *Abraham Lincoln* in May 2003 to tell the world that "major combat operations in Iraq have ended," Time Books published a glossy hardback called *21 Days to Baghdad: The Inside Story of How America Won the War Against Iraq*. The book concludes with a photo of the president posing on the deck of the *Abraham Lincoln* in that snug flight suit. Although it includes one horrific image of Ali Ismail Abbas, a twelve-year-old Baghdad boy who lost both arms and his family to a U.S. missile during the invasion, the book is an oddly sanitized thing, a slick postcard from a short and tightly scripted war. The triumphant text proclaims that the V-J Day moment in Iraq occurred "on April 9, when a U.S. team tied a chain to a statue of Saddam in Baghdad's Paradise Square and, with a couple of hefty yanks, pulled it from its pedestal."

21 Days to Baghdad is a time capsule in a way, and since its publication it has come to emit a whiff of rot. It is a reminder of how reportorial curiosity can surrender to patriotic stagecraft and, in turn, how such stagecraft can shield political decision-making from skepticism at moments when skepticism is most needed. The book is both innocent and cynical.

In August 2004, after starkly different images had circulated around the world—from footage of the suicide bombing of the United Nations headquarters in Baghdad in August 2003 and the killing of four U.S. contractors in Fallujah in March 2004 to the snapshots of American forces abusing Iraqis at Abu Ghraib prison—and as the tactics of various militias and insurgent groups, along with the efforts of occupation forces to contain them, was making daily life in many parts of Iraq perilous, the *Columbia Journalism Review* asked Farnaz Fassihi, a Baghdad-based reporter at *The Wall Street Journal*, to keep a diary of her time in country. She agreed, but before we could print her piece we were scooped, inadvertently, by Fassihi herself. Fassihi was in the habit of sending periodic e-mails about her life in Baghdad to a circle of family and friends, and in her September 2004 note, roughly the length of a long op-ed piece, she explained her darkening mood. "Being a foreign correspondent in Baghdad these days is like being under virtual house arrest," she wrote:

> I leave when I have a very good reason to and a scheduled interview. I avoid going to people's homes and never walk in the streets. I can't go grocery shopping any more, can't eat in restaurants, can't strike a conversation with strangers, can't look for stories, can't drive in any thing but a full armored car, can't go to scenes of breaking news stories, can't be stuck in traffic, can't speak English outside, can't take a road trip, can't say I'm an American, can't linger at checkpoints, can't be curious about what people are saying, doing, feeling. And can't and can't.

Fassihi went on to say that "the genie of terrorism, chaos, and mayhem has been unleashed onto this country as a result of American mistakes."

Somehow the e-mail got beyond Fassihi's circle, and it was forwarded and forwarded around the world until it became a public document. Among fellow journalists the reaction was swift and varied: some worried that an objective reporter had dropped her guard; others felt she was suggesting that no worthwhile reporting could be done in Iraq; still others thought her e-mail's grim depiction of a journalist's working life in Baghdad—a daily agenda of can'ts—was accurate, and that the authority of her eyewitness account had communicated the reality of what Iraqis call "the situation" more forcefully than column upon column of standard newspaper prose.

We wanted more. In spring 2006 we hired three experienced war reporters—Vivienne Walt, based in Paris; Judith Matlofff, in New York City; and Christopher Allbritton, in Beirut—and asked them to interview Fassihi and a number of other journalists—reporters, photographers, translators, and stringers—who have covered the war in Iraq, and to get them to tell us what it has been like. Walt, Matloff, and Allbritton interviewed forty-six journalists in all, and out of their anecdotes, insights, and photographs (several of which had not been previously published in the U.S.) we composed an oral history—the first of its kind—which was published in the forty-fifth anniversary issue of *Columbia Journalism Review* in November 2006.

This book is an expansion of that magazine story, a longer version created from the same interview transcripts and that, like the magazine article, begins with the invasion of Iraq in March 2003 and ends in late summer 2006. Our decision to stick with these dimensions bears a little explanation. During the year that has passed between the publication of the magazine version of the oral history and its reincarnation in these pages, daily life in Iraq has grown more infernal, the impediments faced by journalists working there have become more treacherous, and the balkanization of the political landscape has become even more severe. "Baghdad is now effectively a dozen cities; they are all at war," Patrick Cockburn reported in the *London Review of Books* in February 2007. "Three and a half years after the U.S. captured Baghdad, it is extraordinary how little of the city it actually controls." (Cockburn, the Baghdad correspondent for the British newspaper *The Independent* and an occasional contributor to the *London Review of Books*, is among the journalists who were interviewed by *CJR*). Our history, we decided, was to an extent a history of how Iraq itself has been torn apart, as seen through the eyes of journalists on the ground as they lived through it. Our interviews of journalists were conducted at a specific time during the war and pertain to a specific era of the war, from its beginning to summer 2006, and we wanted the book to remain as faithful as possible to those conditions. So we decided to add material from the original transcripts and leave our end point unchanged.

The oral history has several interlaced story lines. One is a record of how western journalists began to grasp the growing chasms in Iraq between Americans and Iraqis, between soldiers and civilians, between the Green Zone and the rest of the country, and among Iraqis themselves. Indeed, readers will see that even before Saddam's statue in Firdos Square hit the ground, journalists were picking up signals that America's time in Iraq would be complex, confusing, and worse. Woven into this thread is an account of the impediments—practical, political, professional—that journalists have faced while covering Iraq, and how they have fared in overcoming them. Another strand concerns how individual journalists began to appreciate the deep danger they were in as the occupation wore on and the militias and insurgents took hold, and how they dealt with it.

While reading the interview transcripts we were struck by the fact that the conventions of journalism and the exigencies of reporting this war have sometimes muffled the passion and expertise of particular voices. We wanted to hear the unvarnished stories as well as the stories behind the stories, and, almost always, our interviewees were ready to talk. The journalists who appear in this book have covered what is still the most significant story of our time, and have done so under circumstances that nearly defy belief. We doubt that anyone can read this history without admiring the skill and guts that they bring to the job, their stubborn effort to get the story right despite the obstacles. They have lived and studied "the situation" closely, some of them for four years or more. Many of them have been in Iraq longer than a fair number of soldiers, diplomats, and aid workers. They know things. This is their story.

Mike Hoyt
John Palattella

New York City
June 2007

Chronology

2003

MARCH 19
U.S.-led coalition
invades Iraq

APRIL 9
U.S. forces occupy
Baghdad; toppling
of Saddam Hussein
statue in Firdos Square

APRIL 21
U.S. establishes
Coalition Provisional
Authority (CPA)
as transitional
government

MAY 1
President George
W. Bush's "Mission
Accomplished" speech
on the deck of the
USS *Abraham Lincoln*

MAY 6
Paul Bremer
appointed CPA
administrator

MAY 23
Iraqi Army disbanded

JULY 13
Iraqi Governing
Council (IGC),
composed of twenty-
five Iraqi nationals
chosen by U.S.-led
coalition, meets to
begin drafting new
constitution

AUGUST 19
UN offices bombed,
killing UN envoy
Sergio Vieira de Mello
and twenty-one others;
UN begins to remove
staff from Iraq

AUGUST 29
A car bomb in Najaf
kills Shia leader
Ayatollah Mohammed
Baqr al-Hakim and
scores of others near
the Tomb of Ali, a
Shia shrine

OCTOBER 27
First day of Ramadan:
suicide attacks kill
more than thirty-four
and wound hundreds
at Red Cross HQ and
four Baghdad police
stations

DECEMBER 14
Saddam Hussein
captured near Tikrit

2004

JANUARY 28
David Kay, former
head of Iraq Survey
Group, testifies
before Senate Armed
Services Committee
that he found no
evidence that Iraq
had stockpiled
unconventional
weapons before
U.S.-led invasion

FEBRUARY 1
During Eid
celebrations, suicide
bombings of the
offices of the main
Kurdish political
parties in Irbil kill at
least a hundred
Kurds

MARCH 1

IGC agrees on a temporary constitution, which recognizes Islamic law as a source of legislation

MARCH 2

Attacks across Iraq on Ashura , a Shiite holy day, kill more than a hundred people. U.S. officials blame Abu Musab al-Zarqawi, who they claim has links to al-Qaeda

MARCH 31

Four U.S. contractors killed in Fallujah. Their mutilated bodies are hung from a bridge with a sign stating "Fallujah is the cemetery for Americans"

APRIL 4

Shia uprisings in several cities after the arrest of an aide to Moqtada al-Sadr and the closure of al-Sadr's newspaper. An arrest warrant for al-Sadr is issued

APRIL 5

U.S. forces surround Fallujah at the start of an operation to pacify insurgents

APRIL 21

Four suicide attacks aimed at police buildings in Basra leave at least sixty-eight dead

APRIL 28

Images of abuse and torture at Abu Ghraib appear worldwide

APRIL 30

U.S. troops pull back from Fallujah

MAY 17

President of IGC, Ezzedine Salim, is killed by suicide bomber at a checkpoint outside the Green Zone

MAY 21

Spanish troops withdraw from Iraq

MAY 26

The New York Times admits that its coverage of the administration's claims about Iraq's WMD capabilities was "not as rigorous as it should have been"

MAY 28

Iyad Allawi named interim prime minister

JUNE 28

Bremer transfers sovereignty to Iraq. CPA dissolved, Allawi and his cabinet sworn in

JULY 7

Allawi signs a law allowing for martial law to be imposed in troubled regions, as Iraqis are increasingly killed in insurgent attacks

JULY 15

Philippine troops begin to leave Iraq to save life of Filipino hostage

AUGUST 7

Allawi government orders the closure of the Baghdad office of Al-Jazeera

AUGUST 18

One-hundred-seat National Assembly selected by Iraqi National Conference

AUGUST 27

Najaf forces loyal to al-Sadr leave the Imam Ali Mosque after three weeks of fighting U.S. forces. The truce is brokered by Shia leader Ayatollah Ali Sistani

OCTOBER 6

A CIA report authored by Charles Duelfer, who succeeded David Kay as the head of the Iraq Survey Group, states that Iraq's WMD program was essentially destroyed in 1991 Gulf War, and Saddam ended Iraq's nuclear program after 1991

OCTOBER 24

Forty-nine unarmed Iraqi Army recruits are ambushed and executed

NOVEMBER 2

Bush reelected

NOVEMBER 7

U.S. troops launch offensive to retake Fallujah. Allawi declares martial law

2005

NOVEMBER 8
U.S. launches all-out assault on Fallujah

NOVEMBER 15
U.S. says its troops control Fallujah and have killed 1,200 insurgents

DECEMBER 21
Fourteen U.S. soldiers killed by suicide bombing at a U.S. military base in Mosul

JANUARY 12
WMD search is declared over by U.S. inspectors

JANUARY 30
Iraqis vote in first multiparty elections

APRIL 7
Kurdish leader Jalal Talabani sworn in as new interim president; Ibrahim al-Jaafari designated new prime minister

MAY 1
Disclosure of Downing Street memo of 7/23/02: "intelligence and facts being fixed around the policy"

MAY 30
U.S. Vice President Dick Cheney claims the insurgency is in its "last throes"

JULY 19
Report by U.K. research groups estimates 25,000 Iraqi civilians killed since 2003

AUGUST 28
Iraqi Sunnis reject constitution

AUGUST 31
Panic spreads over rumors of suicide bombers at a march of Shia faithful during a religious festival; nearly a thousand pilgrims die

OCTOBER 15
Iraqis vote in referendum to ratify draft constitution

OCTOBER 16
U.S. air strikes near Ramadi kill seventy people. U.S. says the dead are militants; local eyewitnesses say most are civilians

OCTOBER 30
In an official published estimate, the Pentagon states that at least 26,000 Iraqis have been killed or injured between January 1, 2004 and September 16, 2005

NOVEMBER 17
U.S. Representative John Murtha (D-Pa.) calls for U.S. troop withdrawal from Iraq

NOVEMBER 22
Daily Mirror publishes a memo revealing that Bush told British Prime Minister Tony Blair during talks in April 2004 that he was considering bombing Al-Jazeera; Blair is said to have talked Bush out of it

DECEMBER 15
Election for a four-year Iraqi government

2006

....

FEBRUARY 22

Two men bomb the al-Askari shrine in Samarra, one of the holiest Shia religious sites. The bombing sparks reprisals against Sunnis

MARCH 19

Time reveals that U.S. Marines allegedly killed at least fifteen unarmed Iraqi civilians in Haditha the previous November

MARCH 30

After eighty-two days of captivity, American journalist Jill Carroll freed by kidnappers

APRIL 21

Nuri Kamal al-Maliki chosen to replace Ibrahim al-Jaafari as Iraq's prime minister

MAY 20

Maliki oversees the formation of Iraq's first permanent constitutional government

JUNE 7

Abu Musab al-Zarqawi killed in a U.S. air raid

JUNE 20

Mutilated bodies of two U.S. soldiers found in Youssifiyah

JULY 3

U.S. soldier charged with rape and murder of a young Iraqi girl in March 2005 in Mahmudiya, south of Baghdad

AUGUST 3

Head of U.S. Central Command, General John Abizaid, suggests civil war is possible in Iraq

AUGUST 16

The New York Times reports that 1,666 bombs exploded in Iraq in July, the highest monthly total to date

SEPTEMBER 20

UN report estimates that hundreds more Iraqis died in violence in July and August than in the previous two months (May/June: 5,818; July: 3,590; August: 3,009)

SEPTEMBER 21

Italian troops withdraw from Iraq, handing control of Dhi Qar province to Iraqi troops

SEPTEMBER 26

Release of the partly declassified April 2006 National Intelligence Estimate on "Trends in Global Terrorism," which states that "the Iraq conflict has become the 'cause célèbre' for jihadists, breeding a deep resentment of U.S. involvement in the Muslim world and cultivating supporters for the global jihadist movement"

NOVEMBER 7

Democrats win control of Senate and House of Representatives in U.S. elections

DECEMBER 30

Saddam Hussein executed by hanging after being found guilty of crimes against humanity by the Iraqi Special Tribunal

The Journalists

This oral history knits together excerpts from interviews with forty-four journalists. Noted below are the periods during which these journalists have reported on the war from Iraq and the media organizations for whom they have worked while in country (unless otherwise indicated) through June 2007 (the "present").

HANNAH ALLAM
REPORTER
KNIGHT RIDDER
(McCLATCHY)
July 2003–September 2005

CHRISTOPHER ALLBRITTON
FREELANCE WRITER, BLOGGER
TIME, Back to Iraq
March 2003–present

GHAITH ABDUL-AHAD
REPORTER, PHOTOGRAPHER
THE GUARDIAN,
GETTY IMAGES
March 2003–present

DEBORAH AMOS
FOREIGN CORRESPONDENT
NPR
May 2003–present

JON LEE ANDERSON
STAFF WRITER
THE NEW YORKER
February 2003–present

JANE ARRAF
SENIOR BAGHDAD CORRESPONDENT
CNN
March 2003–present

LUKE BAKER
BAGHDAD BUREAU CHIEF
REUTERS
February 2003–December 2005

ANNE BARNARD
REPORTER
THE BOSTON GLOBE
March 2003–December 2005

YOUSIF MOHAMMED BASIL
STRINGER, TRANSLATOR
TIME, CNN
September 2004–present

JOHN BURNS
BAGHDAD BUREAU CHIEF
THE NEW YORK TIMES
October 2002–May 2007

ANDREW LEE BUTTERS
FREELANCE WRITER
NEW YORK SUN, PEOPLE, TIME
October 2003–July 2004

THANASSIS CAMBANIS
REPORTER
THE BOSTON GLOBE
March 2003–December 2005

RAJIV CHANDRASEKARAN
REPORTER, BAGHDAD BUREAU CHIEF
THE WASHINGTON POST
March 2003–October 2004

PATRICK COCKBURN
REPORTER
THE INDEPENDENT (LONDON)
March 2003–present

BORZOU DARAGAHI
REPORTER
LOS ANGELES TIMES
September 2002–present

WILLIAM DARLEY
FORMER U.S. ARMY PUBLIC
AFFAIRS OFFICER, EDITOR IN CHIEF
*MILITARY REVIEW: THE PROFESSIONAL
JOURNAL OF THE U.S. ARMY*
August 2003–March 2004

THOMAS DWORZAK
PHOTOGRAPHER
MAGNUM PHOTO
October 2002–December 2005

RICHARD ENGEL
CORRESPONDENT
NBC NEWS
February 2003–present

ALI FADHIL
TRANSLATOR, REPORTER
NPR, *FINANCIAL TIMES,*
THE GUARDIAN, THE NEW YORKER
October 2003–January 2006

FARNAZ FASSIHI
REPORTER
THE WALL STREET JOURNAL
January 2003–December 2005

DEXTER FILKINS
REPORTER
THE NEW YORK TIMES
March 2003–August 2006

ANNE GARRELS
CORRESPONDENT
NPR
October 2002–present

MARCELA GAVIRIA
PRODUCER
FRONTLINE
July 2003–December 2006

PATRICK GRAHAM
FREELANCE WRITER
OBSERVER (LONDON),
*NATIONAL POST, THE NEW YORK TIMES
MAGAZINE, THE GUARDIAN,
OUTSIDE, HARPER'S,* CBC RADIO
November 2002–September 2004

CAROLINE HAWLEY
CORRESPONDENT
BBC
April 2003–December 2005

JAMES HIDER
REPORTER
THE TIMES (LONDON)
May 2003–present

PAUL HOLMES
EDITOR, POLITICAL AND GENERAL NEWS
REUTERS (BASED IN NEW YORK CITY)
September 2002–present

CHRIS HONDROS
PHOTOGRAPHER
GETTY IMAGES
March 2003–present

LARRY KAPLOW
REPORTER
COX NEWSPAPERS
March 2003–present

TOM LASSETER
REPORTER
KNIGHT RIDDER (McCLATCHY)
March 2003–February 2007

PETER MAASS
CONTRIBUTING WRITER
THE NEW YORK TIMES MAGAZINE
March 2003–April 2005

GEORGES MALBRUNOT
REPORTER
LE FIGARO
February 2003–December 2004

DAN MURPHY
REPORTER, BAGHDAD BUREAU CHIEF
THE CHRISTIAN SCIENCE MONITOR
September 2003–December 2006

ROBERT NICKELSBERG
CONTRACT PHOTOGRAPHER
TIME
March 2003–present

ELIZABETH PALMER
CORRESPONDENT
CBS NEWS
December 2002–present

SCOTT PETERSON
REPORTER, PHOTOGRAPHER
THE CHRISTIAN SCIENCE MONITOR,
GETTY IMAGES
September 2002–present

MITCH PROTHERO
REPORTER
UNITED PRESS INTERNATIONAL
April 2003–present

NIR ROSEN
FREELANCE WRITER
TIME, ASIA TIMES, THE PROGRESSIVE,
PITTSBURGH POST-GAZETTE, THE NEW YORKER,
THE NEW YORK TIMES MAGAZINE
March 2003–present

ALISSA RUBIN
REPORTER, BAGHDAD BUREAU CHIEF
LOS ANGELES TIMES
April 2003–present

ANTHONY SHADID
REPORTER
THE WASHINGTON POST
March 2003–present

LIZ SLY
REPORTER
CHICAGO TRIBUNE
March 2003–present

MARTIN SMITH
PRODUCER
FRONTLINE
April 2003–December 2006

VIVIENNE WALT
FREELANCE WRITER
USA Today, Time, The Boston Globe
September 2002–present

NANCY YOUSSEF
BAGHDAD BUREAU CHIEF
KNIGHT RIDDER (McCLATCHY)
April 2003–January 2007

An Iraqi mother comforts her two-year-old son at the Saddam Hospital in Tikrit, where the child was recovering from injuries caused by shrapnel when their house was hit during a U.S.-led coalition bombing raid. April 17, 2003. Reuters/Jerry Lampen/Landov

I

IN THE BEGINNING

DEXTER FILKINS | *THE NEW YORK TIMES*

If you look at the whole arc of this thing, it used to be easy in the beginning, but it was never easy. I remember literally the first day I went into Iraq, and it was the day of the invasion. I drove in on my own; I was one of a very small handful of people that actually got across the border in Kuwait. And I was what the American military called a unilateral [laughing], which is, I just had my own car. I think it took about twelve hours that day to find my way across the border into Iraq. In the invasion I was on my own completely; I had an Arabic translator and I had a photographer, and we made our way to Baghdad by ourselves, basically, and it was pretty insane, and I probably wouldn't do it again.

I remember, literally the first day, driving into Safwan, which is the first town on the border when you cross over. It's where they signed the surrender in 1991. And I went in there thinking that this is probably going to be something like what I saw in Afghanistan, which was cheering crowds and people throwing their turbans off, and everybody happy to see the American forces. And that wasn't the case at all. To me, it looked like we'd pried the doors off a mental institution, and there were a bunch of people standing around with their jaws hanging open. Some people were absolutely horrified, people were crying, some people were cheering, some people were—you could tell how afraid they were. Some people, you could sense that there was emotion that they didn't want to express, so they didn't. There was a lot of uncertainty.

But it was pretty scary, too. I remember that moment when I arrived in Safwan: the great concern of many of the people there—they were all Shiites—was that there were secret police all over the place, and as soon as the Americans left, the secret police were going to come in and arrest everybody and kill them. So everyone was totally horrified and really afraid to talk to us, and it was really, really dangerous because there were Iraqi Army people all over the place, and there were guys taking their uniforms off, there were tanks up the road and stuff going off, and it was really, really crazy, and it wasn't anything like Afghanistan. I mean, Afghanistan was like a tea party compared to Iraq, just in terms of size and just insanity. Iraq was just orders of magnitude greater. Whatever expectations that I brought in across the border that day, I just chucked immediately because it was totally different. It was clear immediately that it was going to be a lot harder to work. It really was.

PETER MAASS |
THE NEW YORK TIMES MAGAZINE
The marines took a bridge [on the way to Baghdad], and then took the other side of the bridge, and seized the road that went from Baghdad to the bridge, and they set up a perimeter. And unfortunately, because this road was actually an escape route for civilians who were trying to leave Baghdad, there were cars that came up the road to leave Baghdad

by the bridge that the marines had just taken. And, because the marines had not been able to drive vehicles over the bridge, because the bridge was damaged, civilians who were driving up the road to flee Baghdad over the bridge did not see any American military vehicles and thought, "Fine, it's safe," because the marines were dug in, into camouflage positions, setting up their new perimeter on this road. So what happened was, civilian vehicles drove up this road, and the marines shot them up.

I was two hundred or three hundred meters back. The road bends just a little bit, and there are some small houses and stores on the side of the road. So I could not see what was happening down the road. I was with the commander. I knew that there were vehicles coming up and they were taken care of. We assumed they were all military vehicles. Or ordinary vehicles carrying Republican Guard or whatever, because, you know, we didn't really know the situation. But the marines, particularly the snipers who were on the front line, who were looking through scopes and could see faces in vehicles, knew what was going on. And the photographers were there. So, the photographers heard the sniper commanders saying, "Don't shoot, don't shoot." The snipers would fire to disable the vehicles, hit the engine block, hit the tire so the vehicle can't go forward. Even though the orders were, let the snipers handle it, when the marines, the ordinary grunts, heard one or two shots from a sniper, they'd all open up.

So, you had all these civilians, women and children, getting killed on that road.

[In the morning] I just kind of walked down there and looked at the vehicles and saw the civilian bodies. And on the side of the road there were a couple of civilians who were burying the bodies, and one of them spoke a little bit of English. He had been in one of the vehicles and told me what had happened. And so I was able to see with my own eyes the result of what had happened. I was able to see dead civilians, cars along this road that were shot full of holes, the bodies were still there, and there were witnesses there. The title of the story in *The New York Times Magazine* was "Good Kills," because the battalion commander, [Lieutenant Colonel] Bryan McCoy, when I was with him during the battle, I had asked him, "How are things going?" And he had a cigar at that moment, I think, and he said, "Oh, you know, it's a day of good kills." And that, "good kills," is kind of a military term that officers and soldiers will use, meaning their job is to kill people, the right people. But he didn't know, at that time he didn't know that there were civilians being killed.

He did realize afterwards. And a lot of people in that battalion knew, not just the ones who shot those vehicles. And I think, actually, when they were shooting, they didn't know whether there were civilians in them or not, they were just scared. There was one marine who I quoted in the story, who was on the road checking out the bodies. And one of the photographers was with me at that moment, and the photographer was saying, not in a whisper, "This should not have happened. This was wrong." And, this particular marine heard that and swore, said something. So I went up to him and said, "Well, what do you think about what happened?"—because he was amid all the bodies, as I was—and he kind of said, "Look, you know, you can't second-guess it. We've got to keep ourselves safe. We didn't know who was in the vehicles. This is war, and this is what happens in war." And so I put that in, paraphrasing his words, into the story. Two days later, Baghdad falls. This battalion, by the way, was the battalion that took down the statue of Saddam.

DEXTER FILKINS | *THE NEW YORK TIMES*
This is during the invasion, and I was hanging out with some soldiers and these two very young guys came back, and their eyes were burning, they were really, really pumped up. They'd just been in a big firefight, and I remember—I can't remember the guy's name—he said, "Yeah, we were just mowing people down. We were just whacking people." And I said, "Are the insurgents mixing in with civilians?" And he said, "Yeah, and we just shot the civilians too." And I remember he said this remarkable thing. He was describing some woman who had kind of stepped in front of—the insurgent had stepped behind her, so he said, yeah, he shot this woman, and he said, "The chick got in the way," and so he killed her. He wasn't especially troubled by it.

He was annihilated when that thing ran the next morning. I was amazed: Here it is the middle of full-on combat; all of his officers had read the story by the next morning; and from their tent they chewed him out to no end. They summoned me to the tent and chewed me out. I just said, "Hey, you know, deal with it. That's what he said and that's what happened." And I wasn't embedded, so they were perfectly free to kick me out and they made that clear, and I said something like, "Okay, do what you got to do, but I'm not going to pull punches, I'm going to write what I see." So they talked about it and they said, "Okay, you can stay." So they probably weren't as accommodating after that as they might have been. I remember Oliver North was flying in and out and meeting with all these officers, and I remember I was trying to get an interview with the colonel who was in charge of this unit and I couldn't get anywhere near him after that. And Ollie North was flying in and out and they were sort of rolling out a red carpet for him. But I don't know, I didn't get kicked out, you know?

PAUL HOLMES | REUTERS
The first killing of a Reuters journalist was on April the eighth 2003, which was the day before Baghdad fell, and the man killed was a Ukrainian Reuters cameraman, Taras Protsyuk. He and a Spanish cameraman for Telecinco, José Couso, were killed when a U.S. tank opened fire on the Palestine Hotel, which was where all the journalists had moved in the course of the war—and it was known that that was the hotel where the international media was staying. The U.S. military at first, on the day of the killing, in which two of our journalists were also wounded, argued that there were armed men in the Palestine Hotel and that there was an Iraqi spotter who was directing fire at this unit, this [U.S. Army unit] which was on a bridge in Baghdad and was coming under fire. Now the question at the time was why didn't the military on the ground know that this was the Palestine Hotel, and it was therefore a neutral building?

And what happened was that there was an Iraqi spotter somewhere, who was speaking over a radio, that was being listened into by the Americans—they'd captured another radio, so they could listen to communications from the spotter. But one of the men in the [U.S. M1A1 Abrams] tank saw this glint from a high floor of the Palestine Hotel and concluded that that was the spotter, and the tank received permission to open fire. The U.S. ultimately backed down from—or kept changing its story, but in the end they said that the soldiers' actions were justified under the rules of engagement, it was tragic but it happened. We never got access to their investigation. As far as I'm aware, people at the Palestine Hotel were never questioned. Journalists in the hotel were never questioned by the U.S. military in the course of their investigation. And the only way we—Reuters—got hold of their investigation report—a redacted version, in other words, with bits censored—was through the CPJ

[Committee to Protect Journalists], which got it under the Freedom of Information Act.

RICHARD ENGEL | NBC

I first went to Baghdad in 2001. It was Saddam's referendum, the election where he got 100 percent of the vote, and then I went back a couple of other times when it became clear that the war was about to happen and all the troops were being positioned, and everyone was talking war and there were deadlines coming up at the UN. A lot of reporters were heading to Baghdad, and the Information Ministry was in a bit of a crisis; they were trying to regulate who was there. The big networks were trying to divvy up their visas so that their future television stars and print stars could be made, and it was a very confusing time for the government in Iraq, which was in a bit of a state of panic. I think Iraq didn't expect that this war would actually happen. A lot of the government officials that I spoke to thought, "Nah, it's not going to happen." Senior government officials in Iraq thought that the war would just blow over, and that all of this was just saber-rattling and that in the end maybe there'd be a couple of cruise missile strikes, but they didn't think that there'd be a real ground war.

Then access increased dramatically for me. When it became clear that this war was about to happen, and it was going to be totally unpredictable, and there was talk of chemical weapons and there was talk of the mother of all bombs, the MOAB, and there was talk of electronic pulse weapons—people blinked. CNN was thrown out, Fox was never allowed in the country to begin with—they hated Fox. ABC, CBS, NBC, and many print organizations basically pulled their people out. They said we're not willing to take casualties like that, and it left a space for some reporters who were able to just be there on like an illegal visa, a human shield visa, and there was a small group of people who were there that left. And so suddenly our access became much better because the Iraqis woke up to the fact that this war's about to happen and no one's going to cover it. Suddenly they became much more available. We were meeting government ministers, they were trying to take us on organized bus tours, they were trying to show us their version of the war.

We all had multiple hotel rooms. There were all sorts of games. We didn't know what was going to happen, so I had a hotel room at the Hamra Hotel, I had apartments, I had a safe house set up in a garage. The [local] pharmacist said that if things went badly I could stay with him. I had another hotel called The Dulaimi—a room set up there. I hired a police officer, a corrupt police officer and put him up at the hotel. In case things went badly I figured I would need somebody with a badge, if there were checkpoints and things like that.

We all got heavy minders. Since I spoke Arabic I got a pretty senior minder, and at this stage I was the only person reporting for television. So the minders at first were all over us. And then as the war progressed, a lot of them just got scared, and my minder at one stage just stopped coming: just disappeared. I think he went home, just went to his village. A lot of Iraqis just went home, just decided they weren't going to show up for work. A lot of the soldiers just didn't show up for work, didn't show up for battle. And that was also good and bad, because having the minder also gave you a degree of protection. For example, one day I tried to shake my minder, I went out the back door and started doing interviews on the street. Baath Party officials came and arrested me and I was going to be thrown in jail during the war by the Baath Party, which would not have been a good situation. Luckily, I talked my way out of it and they sent me back with a stern warning: don't do this again. So at least if you had a minder, it was a degree of protection in uncertain times from the government; you were less likely to be taken and arrested.

So the access was at first controlling, and then the system disintegrated, and then in the end it totally disintegrated, and it was amazing. On April 8, it just fell apart. There was just no government anymore. All the government press conferences stopped. All the people in the hotel, the minder—gone. The government was just as if it had never existed.

LARRY KAPLOW | COX NEWSPAPERS
I remember the day [April 9] the Americans came into Baghdad, and I was standing by the side of the street watching the convoy go by. And some of the Humvees had little

American flags on the antennas, just a couple of them. An Iraqi ophthalmologist—there were two from the eye center nearby—saw me going to the crowd and they spoke some English. And they said to me, "Look, you've got to tell them to take these flags off the Humvees. They're going to make people so mad." And I said, "Well, what makes you mad about it?" And he said, "They're Americans and that's the American flag. That's what occupiers do. That's an occupation and that's what people don't want here." And I think a lot of us picked up on the first day a lot of very ambivalent feelings, and those feelings were basically completely overwhelmed by the images and, most important, the superficial event that took place that day—the statue being taken down, the Americans taking control of the city.

ANNE GARRELS | NPR
The toppling of statue—yes, there were people celebrating, but there were as many people standing in shock. It was not just one big party, as I think the cameras tried to make it out to be. In fact, *Morning Edition* called me after the first feed, and they were seeing the TV coverage, and said, "Do you want to redo it for the next feed, because it seems like the pictures are people celebrating." And I said, "Well, there are so few people trying to pull down the statue that they can't do it themselves; the marines have had to intervene, rightly or wrongly, with a crane to pull it down." Many people were just sort of standing, hoping for the

A statue of Saddam Hussein is felled in
central Baghdad. April 9, 2003.
Goran Tomasevic/Reuters/Landov

best, but they weren't joyous; there was a very mixed feeling about seeing American soldiers in their midst.

And there was a quote. A man was standing next to me, a university professor, by pure chance, and he said to me, "You understand, you will now have to be in complete control, and we will resent you every step of the way." And he was so right. The only problem was that of course the U.S. was never in complete control and the resentment was probably even greater because of it.

PETER MAASS |
THE NEW YORK TIMES MAGAZINE

There was this one guy in the crowd who I started talking to, watching the statue being taken down, and he spoke very good English, and he was just nice. And I asked him who was he and all that stuff, and he had been staying in the Sheraton. And he was saying "I'm so glad the statue's coming down," blah, blah, blah. The next day, this guy, I was watching, outside the Sheraton, somebody started pointing at him and saying something. Apparently he was a friend of Saddam's, or a Sunni of some sort. And somebody who was an opponent of the regime saw him and tried to kill him, and marines had to intervene to save this guy's life. But a lot of people were around him shouting and spitting and saying, "This guy's a bad guy." So I think there were people like that. This guy, for example, who I was standing next to, talking to, who was saying, "Oh, this is a great day for Baghdad," blah,

blah, blah. Actually, he was a Baathist of some sort, and he was a very smart Baathist, and he was saying what he thought needed to be said at that moment in order to kind of guarantee his safety. So not everybody who was in that square watching was genuinely enthusiastic and was an opponent of the regime. This one guy in particular who told me, "Oh, this is great. This guy was horrible." It turns out that he was some kind of pro-regime guy, and so he was just kind of participating in this thing.

THANASSIS CAMBANIS |
THE BOSTON GLOBE

The day we arrived in Iraq, the security threat was getting hit by stray bullets. The most dangerous thing that happened to me that first week in Baghdad [around April 11, 2003] was a sniper hit the window behind where I was working, about a foot and a half from the back of my head; I was acting like the danger was past when in fact there were these little bits of fighting going on. Once that ended after the first week, I felt no safety constraints whatsoever, partly out of ignorance and partly I felt there was no one out there who had it in for us. In fact, for that first month I felt incredibly safe around Baghdad. The kinds of crime we saw were people in a neighborhood trying to blast open the wall in a bank vault and steal all the money in it because there was no bank staff and no police. So really the first couple weeks the sky was the limit, there were no obstacles, security obstacles whatsoever.

LARRY KAPLOW | COX NEWSPAPERS

You were coming across American soldiers who looked like they'd just beamed down from a spacecraft, and had no idea which way was which and what they were doing and who they should be looking out for, and at the same time were mingling with Iraqis on foot, and stopping in juice shops for drinks.

JANE ARRAF | CNN

It was a free-for-all in every sense of the word. Along with the unrestrained looting and the chaos that that implied, there were also enormous possibilities to do all kinds of reporting. And if you had a bureau there, like we did, and it was a known bureau and a known company like CNN was, it was a beacon for everybody. It was a beacon for Iraqis who believed they had stories. Iraqis would show up, there would be Iraqis lined up outside the door. There would be the Iraqis who needed medicine for their dying mothers, there would be the Iraqis who told you they had nuclear documents in their basement and would you like to come and look. You know, there was almost that pang when you turned somebody away, [you were] thinking, "Damn, maybe this guy really does have nuclear weapons in his basement, but I don't have time." So you never really knew. And then there would be the line for the American soldiers who hadn't talked to their family in six months. Everywhere you went, because we had satellite phones, there would be people desperate, desperate, desperate to get in touch with their families.

NIR ROSEN | FREELANCE WRITER

My first day there [April 13, 2003], I had a driver, a Shia driver, drive me around, and he took me to Sadr City, which at the time was still called Saddam City. But the event that had a lasting effect on me was a week later—going to a Sunni mosque in the al Adhamiya district. I was actually going there just to meet an old college friend who was in Baghdad and I thought I would catch up with her. She was at the mosque. Iraq's most important Sunni cleric had just gotten back from five years of exile, and about ten thousand people had come to hear him speak. He was comparing the Americans to Mongols—the Mongols had sacked Baghdad in 1258 and now the new Mongols were in Iraq—and he was emphasizing Sunni-Shia unity [and] opposition to the Americans from the first day, the importance of the mosque to thousands of Iraqis as the only place where there was any real political discourse or leadership or authority.

And these marines—a patrol of marines walked in on the whole event—on the Friday service with ten thousand people there—and this was like the most pro-Saddam neighborhood in Baghdad—wealthy Sunni Baathists. They walked right into the crowd on the street, and there was a very tense standoff. They were pointing their machine guns at the crowd. The crowd was very angry.

And they were very arrogant, the soldiers. [The people in the mosque] were very terrified and they asked me to explain to [the soldiers'] officer that it wasn't a good time to be there, to ask them to leave. It was Friday prayers, people were angry, so I went up to the officer and I told him, "Hey man, it's Friday prayers, people are angry, you shouldn't be here," and he told me something like, "I don't care, that's why we've got the guns." It looked like there was about to be a massacre; it was so tense that it was amazing that it ended peacefully—they just walked away. The crowd was very, very angry.

The movement that arose from that guy's arrival, Dr. Kubeisi [Sheikh Ahmad al Kubeisi], would eventually become the Association of Muslim Scholars. This was an attempt to find Sunni leadership and a Sunni voice because there was none. It was much easier for the Shias because Shia clerics had more authority and there were a few key Shia clerics who went up against the authority. And Sunni clerics just don't have the same importance for Sunnis that Shia clerics have for Shias, so it was much harder for the Sunnis, and the association was one attempt to create a Sunni block, because they realized they were weak compared to the Shias.

RICHARD ENGEL | NBC NEWS

It was very chaotic and you could walk the streets and people you know wanted to show you things, people had never been able to speak before. I'd been in Iraq for a couple of months at this stage, but I'd never been able to walk the streets and talk to people for fear of getting them in deep trouble or getting myself into an uncomfortable situation. So

I was just able to walk around and talk to people and they were showing you into their houses and they were finding documents— everyone was looting the government buildings and finding the files—[Saddam Hussein's government] had secret files on them, and they were finding out that their neighbors had been informing on them for years. Some of the problems that we're still suffering from were already becoming evident at this stage: all of the rage and mismanagement, frustration and anger.

A perfect anecdote: I read it in a local newspaper and chased it down and it was a true story. In Basra there was a farmer and he had a small herd of cows—let's say four or five cows. In the late nineties, this farmer had gone to the local office of the Ministry of Agriculture and had asked for some medicine because one of his cows had some sort of illness. And, you know, typical, disorganized, inefficient government—they said no, come back, go to a different office, they gave him a bit of a runaround, and all of his cows died, and his livelihood was destroyed. And these kinds of things happen. Right after the war, this farmer, we're talking five years later, went back and found that local government official, and said, "You owe me four cows, plus interest, or I'm going to kill you." The guy didn't have the money, or said he didn't have the money, and he was killed. There was a sense of euphoria and opportunity, but there was also the opportunity to get even.

LARRY KAPLOW | COX NEWSPAPERS

I had been blacklisted, or wasn't able to get a visa [from the Iraqi government] for about a year and a half, from the middle of 1999 to 2001.

There were some guys who didn't like things I'd written from Kurdistan in early 1999, which I know because after the fall of the government a friend of mine was in the Ministry of Information looking through all the debris and found my actual file and gave it to me. It had some notes on some articles I had written about how I was writing bad things against the government of Iraq.

Actually I did a little column on it. They're mostly kind of notes in margins. It was very unsophisticated—they were getting my clips out of things like *The Washington Times*, which had picked them up from the wire service and run them. They didn't appear to be checking the Internet or getting it out of our actual Cox papers.

RAJIV CHANDRASEKARAN |
THE WASHINGTON POST

I was one of the first reporters into the Baghdad Museum. I saw rooms that had been stripped bare. I saw people with crowbars running in to pry open cases. It would become clear later that some of those rooms that had been cleared out had actually been cleared out by authorities and stuff had been put into safekeeping. But I also went into supply rooms and saw floors covered in shattered, broken pottery. Some of that stuff would later be judged not to be

incredibly valuable, but some was. Those early reports, I will admit, were, I don't want to say exaggerated, but we didn't know the full scope of things, and we were told by the people there that the losses were greater than they were. Part of the reason was that the people who were there, who worked in the museum, were not privy to the fact that their superiors had taken other items and put them for safekeeping so they think all this stuff had been stolen. But then you have the revisionists saying, "Oh this wasn't very bad at all, there wasn't much gone." The fact of the matter is, there was a lot taken. It was somewhere in the middle. But it was incredibly chaotic, we were trying to sort through it. If I recall correctly, I did not put a specific figure on the losses because it was just hard to really pin it down. It was impossible for anyone to know what had really been taken. But just walking through that museum and seeing it destroyed by looters was heart wrenching. For the first time, I started to think—"We've come here without a plan. It would have taken one tank in front of this building to have protected it, yet we didn't do a single thing to stop it. Did we really sort of come into this with no post-war plan?"

JANE ARRAF | CNN

The day [April 11] that Mosul fell, we were in the palace when it was being looted and it was extraordinary. We walked into the palace and there were no U.S. forces, really nobody in control, and the word had gone out that the Iraqi Army had gone and that the palace was there and it was open. And entire families came. They didn't just come and tour the place. They came and they tore the door hinges off, they came and they took away the marble, and the place was really being dismantled in front of us. We did live shots from there and we did live interviews. And it was an absolutely remarkable thing because it was so unrestrained. That morning we'd gone in thinking, "This is it, this is the end of the Iraqi regime, this is the dawn of a new age." By sundown that day, we had a security guy who was getting really nervous because people were starting to get a little aggressive.

ELIZABETH PALMER | CBS NEWS

There were many unsecured weapons caches in the schools, as I recall, because I think that Iraqi forces at the time thought they would be a good place to hide things because they didn't look very suspect. But the American forces were just overwhelmed, and at that stage nobody—at least not the military—was taking the probability of a really well-equipped and well-organized insurgency properly or seriously, and so there was no feeling that these weapons were being stolen by a group that would become a serious enemy.

JANE ARRAF | CNN

In Mosul, this guy took a knife out from under his shirt and he stabbed this portrait of Saddam, and he stabbed and stabbed and stabbed and slashed at his eyes and I watched this and thought, "Oh my God." I had to remind myself that Saddam is gone. [The man with the knife is] not going to be punished.

RAJIV CHANDRASEKARAN | THE WASHINGTON POST

To me, the real iconic moment wasn't the toppling of any statue, it was this tidal wave of lawlessness. In many ways, that's what then started defining post-Saddam Iraq. Banditry, kidnapping. It sent a signal that everything was fair game. I also think that that really helped to spawn the insurgency when Iraqis who were opposed to the idea of a democratic Iraq realized that if criminals could go around with impunity, then so could they. There was no force, no authority that was going to be placed on them.

LARRY KAPLOW | COX NEWSPAPERS

The chaos went on—people forget—for two months at a high volume, high intensity. Even a month and a half after the fall of the government, people were going around in buses and picking a building, go up there and load up and drive back to Sadr City. And they would dismantle buildings, first of all the valuable and movable things, then the furniture and then the windows and then the window frames and the electrical and the light fixtures and eventually strip the thing bare. This was going on in view of American soldiers, sometimes literally across the street

from where soldiers would be guarding
some of the few places that they were told
to guard. And it was true—and famously or
infamously true—that the Oil Ministry was
one of the few buildings that was guarded
from the very beginning.

ANNE GARRELS | NPR
People were shocked that the U.S. did
nothing, and they will forever remember that
virtually the only building—it wasn't the only
building but one of the few buildings—that
was protected was the Oil Ministry; that
just summed up to so many Iraqis why the
U.S. was there, and confirmed their worst
fears. And it also played to the utter naïveté
of the Americans, because it wasn't just
Iraqis letting off steam, as Rumsfeld said.
It was Baathists going around destroying
documents—making Iraq ungovernable:
destroying drivers' license records, all of the
things that make a city able to be governed.
And it was the beginning of the insurgency.

Mustafa Jassam pretends to be a Saddam Hussein statue
while playing at his aunt's home in Baghdad. He and his
family were forced to move after their home was destroyed
during the initial invasion of Iraq. November 20, 2003.
Andrea Bruce/The Washington Post

II

LIBERTIES AND AMBIGUITIES

CHRIS HONDROS | GETTY IMAGES

Once the fighting stopped, it seemed like the country was getting more pacified. By mid-April or so, all of the most experienced war journalists said, "Okay, now we can do it our way," and, much to the shock and amazement of our embed people, we hired local Iraqis, you know? "Hey, do you have a car?" "Yes, have a car, sir. Yes, no problem." "Okay, come here tomorrow. We'll pay you forty dollars a day." "Okay, yes, no problem." You know, like we normally do in Africa, Asia, anywhere else. That whole first year Iraq was pretty safe to cover, relatively speaking.

ELIZABETH PALMER | CBS NEWS

It was a fool's paradise in a way. I felt we could go anywhere, and we did,

including into the Green Zone, which was extraordinary, because we were able to stroll around Saddam's playground those days and see that crazy canal system where he'd putter around on his little boats.

ANTHONY SHADID |
THE WASHINGTON POST

To me where speaking Arabic was just essential was during the invasion. Because then, during the invasion itself, if you were going to do real reporting, if you were going to do reporting that your colleagues weren't going to be able to do, you had to get rid of your minder. And my minder became a good friend of mine later on. He was complicit in that he did let me go off on my own and do things on my own. But I had to do it in Arabic. And that was essential. I wouldn't have been able to do those stories otherwise.

The Arabic I speak is accented. It's not an Iraqi dialect. And I am treated as a foreigner. I come from a Christian background, which is obvious from the name Anthony. On the one hand, no one is going to take me as an Iraqi. On the other, I think there is, being an Arab-American, and having experience in the region, a kind of shared cultural memory—people expect me to understand what they're talking about.

But it's hard for me to say. I always feel very comfortable in Iraq. And I don't know if that's experience or past or ethnicity or language, but it never felt very alien to me.

DEBORAH AMOS | NPR

I arrived in May of 2003. And I switched jobs to do it. I had been an ABC correspondent and it was very clear to me that I wasn't going to get to go to Baghdad. I had spent a month in Turkey and I got yanked back to New York and so I called up NPR and said I'd be willing to go to Baghdad and I was there within two weeks—no questions asked. I had been to Baghdad in the 1980s and had covered the Iran-Iraq war. And, in fact, had vowed that I would not go back until Saddam was gone because in the '80s and the '90s I was in Kurdistan and knew about the Anfal campaign—that was when that information was first coming out—which was the genocide against the Kurds.

So 2003, I agree, was a paradise for journalists. In the time I had been there before, you couldn't talk to anybody, and now you couldn't get Iraqis to shut up.

Everybody had a story to tell, and they would do it on the record from the rooftops if you let them. And so part of preparing was, could you take the time out to follow your stories when you were so interested in, for example, talking to the people in Basra who had planned the uprising in 1991, and for the first time you could actually find out what happened in 1991. And all of the myths you had heard from that time were not true.

It was, I always thought, remarkable how open Iraqis were to a woman with a tape recorder. It was surprising to me because they had been under such a boot about talking to people and that seemed to wash away very quickly. I think, in part, and as I look back on it now, we spent a great deal of time in Fallujah in those early days because you could go anywhere anytime. People were open to us because there were things that were happening in their community that were already the seeds of the anger that fuels a great deal of what's happening against U.S. troops today. And Iraqis at that time believed that if they told us these things—that they were arrested in the middle of the night, that they were humiliated in front of their children, that U.S. soldiers came in to their wives' bedrooms at three o'clock in the morning—if they told us these things, that somehow it would stop. And they told us and told us and told us and, of course, it didn't stop. There was always a limit to what we could do in our reporting. And remember, in the early days we were up against an incredibly powerful spin machine that accused us of only telling the bad news, and so it was very hard to get that information out.

NIR ROSEN | FREELANCE WRITER

I befriended two American officers who were doing civil affairs and intelligence work. I met them in May of 2003. They were both also Ph.D. students. One of them was getting his Ph.D. in anthropology, and they gave me a room at some point to stay in the Green Zone with the Free Iraqi Forces. I didn't have a place to stay because I had left *Time*, or I'd been told to leave *Time*. You know who the Free Iraqi Forces were? They were Ahmed Chalabi's guys…. I stayed with them at night, but I'd go off and do my own thing during the day—same thing with mosques and stuff. These were the days when Americans could still travel around, so these two officers had an Iraqi driver, put on civilian clothes, and just drove around much of Iraq—the south, much of the north, the Sunni Triangle—and would stay on different bases, and they just brought me along because I was a friend, and they liked having a guy who could go around and look at the Iraqi side of the story. And they were pretty unique as far as Americans went. One of them was reading Benedict Anderson, a book on nationalism, and the other was reading Edward Said. Not the kind of guys you'd expect to be in the American military.

RAJIV CHANDRASEKARAN | *THE WASHINGTON POST*

It wasn't like we were greeted with flowers and sweets, but it was an incredibly warm welcome. I'm fond of saying that back then the greatest risk I felt I was in was being invited into somebody's house and being served food of sketchy origin or tea made from water pumped directly from the Tigris River. When I went up and told people I was an American with *The Washington Post*, I was embraced, I was welcomed into people's homes. They wanted to tell me their stories. These were people who couldn't speak freely, in many cases, for their entire adult lives.

You heard that there was some dustup out in Ramadi or something happening in Al-Qut or Tikrit, you'd just jump in your car and you'd go. You'd take a translator with you, you'd take a granola bar with you and you'd be off. You'd be off in a civilian, soft-skinned vehicle. You wouldn't have to worry about your safety. In those early months, I traveled all over the country. It really wasn't much of a worry. The biggest worries we also faced, aside from the food you were eating, was fuel. It sounds strange to say about a country with the second-largest petroleum reserves—there were a lot of gas stations that weren't working. I remember one trip out, past Fallujah, we actually had to pay people to siphon gasoline out of a bulldozer or a truck. Those were sort of practical concerns, but nobody was worried about roadside bombs, about kidnapping, about being shot at by a sniper, you know, any of that other stuff. It felt so liberating. You really felt like you were on a path to understanding the Iraqi people, understanding their experiences over these past many years of Saddam's government. Chronicling their hopes for the future, and also trying to sort of get a handle on the new political landscape. The political social religious landscape. The growth of the Shia clergy in Najaf. Who was going to move in to take that space? Moqtada al-Sadr and his people? To what degree was Sistani playing a role? The other ayatollahs. The exiles coming back, Chalabi, Iyad Allawi, the Kurdish leadership. Understanding what was happening with the old technocratic ruling class. All these stories, they were incredibly complicated, murky. Of course there were no landline phones, cell phones hadn't been out there. So you were driving to people's homes. There were all these practical constraints on reporting—but you could actually go out there and start scratching the surface on these subjects.

ANTHONY SHADID |
THE WASHINGTON POST

To me, 2003 was really distinctive. It was unusual in a lot of ways. The most unusual was that for the first time, with the possible exception of Lebanon and Palestine, you had an Arab country where you could really try to get a handle on what was going on in the country, try to understand it in a more fundamental way. For so long I had been dealing with information ministries, with censorship, with intimidation, with a certain hesitation to speak. For that period after the fall of Saddam in April 2003, you could

really do any story you wanted as long as you were determined enough, dogged enough, patient enough.

My whole point back then, in 2003, was to do stories on people who'd died, and I was going to reconstruct their lives, the lives of these insurgents who had died, as a way of understanding their motivations, understanding the context, you know, what their agenda, whatever or their inspiration. That worked pretty well, and there were a handful, I think three main stories that I did, including one about a band of five guys who had died in Khaldiya and I had just stumbled onto them because I had seen their picture posted in a barbershop.

At that point in 2003, I was able to visit every one of their families in Khaldiya. I was able to visit the sheikh of the mosque, who basically motivated them to do this, I bought the cassette tapes they were listening to in the local market, and I spent probably three or four solid days in that village just walking up and down the streets. Again, you could do anything you wanted back then if you—not anything, but you could do pretty much anything you needed to do if you were patient enough.

YOUSEF BASIL, TRANSLATOR | *TIME*, CNN

Most of the people in Iraq, they were off the media coverage for a long time. So, they don't really understand, What's the role of the media in Iraqi society? Or what's the role of the media inside the country? So, most of the Iraqi journalists face problems talking to people and making them open up and frankly talk about their problems or some special event that happened or for any accident that might happen there. Most of the people think that media people and most of the journalists—they used to be working with the Iraqi intelligence or with foreign intelligence. They have these ideas, so it's very difficult to talk to people on the street, it's very difficult to convince them that you are just a journalist and you want their story to be published to the world.

SCOTT PETERSON | *THE CHRISTIAN SCIENCE MONITOR*, GETTY IMAGES

I don't suppose there were suddenly revelations in the sense of big surprises or shocks or anything like that, but there were some things that I was expecting that never occurred. For example, I expected that we would be coming across quite substantial warehouses, not of weapons of mass destruction, but of actually well-documented video tapes of torture or human-rights crimes, things like that. Because this was the kind of regime that left a paper trail that was extraordinary. And you saw a taste of this with the huge trail of documentation that was collected from [the Kurdish regions of] northern Iraq during the brief uprising in 1991. In fact, there is even a project at Harvard, their whole job is to go through these 1.8 million documents or whatever it was that were acquired then, and, you know, they documented all kinds of things. And so I was expecting that we would see a lot more

of that.

Now, obviously, there were a lot of intelligence documents and things like that that were found. I was expecting to see an awful lot more actual evidence of crimes, of executions, of things of that nature. And in fact, of course, it wasn't long after the fall of Baghdad that CDs and things were available on the streets showing, you know, the people were buying, showing these things. And it did open the eyes of a lot of Iraqis, if they hadn't been touched by that sort of thing before then they certainly were by the time, shortly after the regime fell. But still, the magnitude of it, it was still just a lot less than I expected, and also a lot less graphic. Because this is the kind of thing that you'd think that Washington, the U.S. military, as a way of justifying the war, they would be the first ones to get this stuff up, get it on Web sites and that sort of stuff. And you know, we just haven't been as horrified as we thought that we would be. I don't think that excuses or explains or indicates that there was less torture or less executions than people thought. It's just that the regime did not record those in the ways that we expected to see.

THANASSIS CAMBANIS | *THE BOSTON GLOBE*

When I came back in July 2003—that was when crime had started. Again, as a western reporter I did not feel at any risk but there was this inescapable criminality around. People were being targeted for money, so

Family farewell lunch sending the sons off to live in a neighboring district with relatives after fears of possible assassination attempts. Photograph by Farah Nosh/Getty Images

again, people's homes were being broken into, people were being carjacked at gunpoint all the time; anyone with a car that wasn't a jalopy carried an AK-47 in order to ward off carjackers. And that was the first major failure of the occupation, and the first sense that it was unsafe in Iraq. We did stories about these gangs. They were like mafia gangs—they were stealing lots of cars and taking them up to Kurdistan and selling them. They were stealing money and doing what you do with stolen money.

ROBERT NICKELSBERG | *TIME*
I started to see [in September 2003], in some of the police training, South African officers—retired, so-called military mercenaries, basically—hired by security companies, contractors. Or Namibian or former Rhodesian people coming in to train the police. I wanted to try and stay long enough to do something with that, but again, the Green Zone became an hour's ordeal just to get inside in order to see somebody, to give you that permission in order to get to those people who may or may not want you around, and that whole routine took a lot of days and time away. I could see it becoming a swamp of approvals and permissions. Again, we were dialing a 914 area code, which is Westchester County [north of New York City], in order to get to speak to somebody inside the Green Zone. How are they doing this? It was faster to send an e-mail to somebody than to speak to somebody on the phone. So I saw that becoming—well, it turned into a need just to be there two months in order to do one

month worth of hard work.

NIR ROSEN | **FREELANCE WRITER**
Right away the Shia clerics—the Shias were the ones who were supposed to welcome the Americans as the liberators—in all of the mosques they were certainly happy that Saddam was gone. But nobody was thanking the Americans. Nobody was greeting them as liberators. Saddam was an authority figure, and authority right away became the mosque. Everything else was wiped out. The vacuum was immediately filled up by the clerics, the tribal leaders, but in Baghdad, mostly clerics. And they were talking about pretty much the same thing: they were warning against the Americans, they were telling the Americans to leave, they were worried about American values corrupting their values—this is what you heard in every single mosque throughout the country.

And the reason I know this is because I started following sermons right away—the Friday sermons—and having friends with other mosques I would have as many samples as I could. One of the reasons why I did this was I realized that this was what Saddam had been doing: I stumbled on to an abandoned security station from one of his intelligence services during, I think, my second week there. And it had been looted but thousands of files were still there, and they had these details, charts for every mosque in town—who was the cleric, what did he say, how many people were there, what kinds of people were there, what were they talking about? The mosque was the only safe place where anybody with authority spoke.

So there were hundreds of political parties that sprung up, but they couldn't say anything except "democracy" and "liberation" and "freedom" and "justice"; that was about all they could say. But in terms of attracting masses of people, there was always the Friday prayers—that was the obvious place to go and talk to people. It might have been a prejudice on my part, but it always where the angriest voices and the loudest voices were heard.

LARRY KAPLOW | COX NEWSPAPERS
In November of 2003 I was supposed to just go do a simple story on troops celebrating Thanksgiving. So I went to a base in Fallujah, and our car broke down within a hundred meters of the base. My translator and I hitchhiked into Fallujah and got a tow truck to pick us up, pick up the car, and then drive us in his tow truck to Baghdad with the car in tow. We knew it was a little dicey and I told my translator, "I won't speak any English, and I can kind of pass myself off as an Iraqi." And we did that, but it was still something you could do in those days. You could just show up in Fallujah and ask for help.

DEXTER FILKINS | *THE NEW YORK TIMES*
We used to go out to dinner at night. It's hard to imagine. I remember one really nice place we used to go called Nabil's. In 2003, we used to go there, not even regularly, but we went there a few times. It was very nice. It was blown up on Christmas Eve of that year. I more or less did anything I wanted. I went into Sunni villages, I met with insurgents, I met with people who hated the United States and you could sit with them and talk about it. You could go out all day in a place like Ramadi—where I think now your life expectancy would be about twenty minutes.

That started to change as the insurgency got going, that was kind of fall 2003. And I remember the day very clearly because I almost didn't survive [laughing]. Ramadan—first day of Ramadan, October 2003—it was about eight o'clock in the morning and we were all having coffee and there was a gigantic bomb blast and it shook our house, it was so close. And it was the ICRC, the International Committee of the Red Cross. Two suicide bombers had hit the place. I actually got there before the cops did, and I remember seeing a suicide bomber—charred remains still clutching the steering wheel—but, you know, bodies everywhere, crowd going insane, as they do.

There were five suicide bombings that day, and I remember hearing the other bombs going off as I was literally walking through the bodies at this place. But we worked there and then drove to another— the second place that had been hit, which was a police station in a neighborhood called Shaab, which is basically a Shiite neighborhood. I stepped out of the car. I was with two photographers. About five hundred people turned on us instantly and surged. I remember there was an old man saying, "Kill them, kill them, kill them!" And so we were grabbed by the crowd and taken by the crowd and they started to beat the hell out of us, and I am reasonably sure they would have killed us, but the driver, my driver—Walid, who's wonderful and happens to be like six-foot-eight and enormous—he reached into the crowd and pulled me out. And we somehow managed to get free and get into the car, and the crowd jumped on the car to try to stop it, which they were pretty close to doing. You know, three hundred people holding a car back could actually do it. They started to throw bricks into the car, and they were smashing the windows, and one of the photographers I was with, Mike Kamber, [they] busted his head open—it was really awful—and we almost didn't get away. I remember we got back, took Mike to the hospital, and later that day we got back to the house, and I remember—I counted them, and I think it was seventeen bricks in the car; every window was smashed out. But that's just an example of how it started to change, and the crowd—I remember the crowd—they blamed us for the bombing, you know? Which didn't make a lot of sense to me—I mean, it doesn't make immediate sense—kind of counterintuitive. But it's like before the Americans got here we didn't have these things and you're American, so we're angry at you.

ANDREW BUTTERS | FREELANCE WRITER

I remember when I first got to Iraq [in October 2003], saw that there was a meeting for American citizens in the convention center to discuss the security precautions which Americans should take in Iraq,

and it was held by a [U.S.] Reserve Army officer, a captain, or a colonel. And after the briefing—which was pretty unremarkable—he realized I'd come in late, and so after the briefing he kind of pulled me aside and asked who I was. And I told him I was a freelance journalist and he said, "Well, you know you're here on your own. Do you have a gun?" And I said, "No! I don't have a gun." And he said, "Well [small chuckle], Why not?" Well, I figured that the other guys would have bigger guns than I'd ever have and they know how to use them. And he said "Get a gun, and learn how to use it."

CAROLINE HAWLEY | BBC

We would drive to Basra. I remember having a picnic on the side of the road for Christmas 2003. We stopped at the side of the road and had tea and eggs after covering Christmas with the British troops.

PATRICK GRAHAM | FREELANCE WRITER

It was hard to find a translator who could work anywhere in Iraq. You wouldn't want—if I went to Sadr City, I would take a translator from Sadr City. But they could sniff, in Sadr City they could sniff a Sunni from the old Baathist elite, and there were a lot of those, the old Ministry of Information people, around, and they could sniff them out very quickly.

I think there were some good translators from the Ministry of Information. Just because you got a job and you needed money and you were willing to report on what journalists were doing, that doesn't necessarily mean that you were by nature an unethical person. Often it was just a matter of survival, and there weren't that many people who spoke English in Iraq, so I think there were some good translators. I mean, there were also the former intelligence people that were being recruited to work as translators, a little iffy.

The real problem was that those people were very good at manipulation. The Baathist regime was—its effect at manipulating was incredible, so you're going into a very dangerous area if you were going, working with them. It was also a case where it was great to work with young translators who were—I thought it was a better idea to work with young translators because suddenly this new world had opened up, and no matter what their allegiance had been before and during the war, where their family allegiances were, they were excited about the future of Iraq, and were far more interested in figuring out what was happening and what their future was.

COLONEL WILLIAM DARLEY |
MILITARY REVIEW
FORMER PUBLIC AFFAIRS OFFICER
Arabic was—language was the Achilles heel, not just of public affairs but of the whole operation. If there's any single lesson for the military in general, all aspects of the military, it's first and foremost the ability to speak to people in their own language. It hampered public affairs to no end, but it was a constant, unremitting problem at every level, every operational level.

There was a survey done at the First Cavalry Division, soon after the arrival of a guy named General Chiarelli, who commanded the First Cavalry Division [as of March 2004], and he brought in every company commander, something like a hundred company commanders. One hundred percent, every company commander in the First Cavalry Division, according to General Chiarelli, every one of them said their number one concern, their number one priority, number one problem they had was language. I mean every one of them, it was unanimous, and that's about as rare as you can get, saying if there was one thing they needed to take with them, that they needed to focus on, was either getting the language ability themselves or taking with them extremely competent linguists. Constant, unremitting problem.

And that problem has shown up constantly across the board in everything. Operational, logistics, you know, intelligence. But in my area, [public affairs], it was just an unremitting problem. Trying to find linguists, trying to find people that were competent. And people you can trust, because if you don't speak the language, you don't really have a great confidence that what is being said is being properly translated, or even nefariously translated. It's a difficult problem if you don't know who you're hiring. You could be hiring a Baathist or somebody who's intentionally there—the Baathists during the Hussein regime are the ones who got privilege. One of those privileges very often was learning foreign languages, advancing in education, and foreign travel. So one of the constant concerns we had is that you run into a guy who speaks very good English, you wonder why. How did this person obtain this level of capability in Saddam Hussein's regime? Very often, that answer would be because he was a high level or privileged official there, and is that a guy you want being hired to be your linguist and translator?

DAN MURPHY |
THE CHRISTIAN SCIENCE MONITOR
We had no concerns whatsoever.
I remember one day I said to our guide, "Look, take off, go home, you've had a long day." Afterwards, I walked up the street for half a mile to go to my favorite sweets shop, and I hopped in a cab and got home. I spoke a hell of a lot less Arabic then than I do now, but that was the way it was then. You know, Iraq has a wonderful road network and we could get up in the morning and think, "Shit, you know what? We haven't been to Mosul in a while, let's go there."
And you drive to Mosul. I mean, I drove to Tal Afar and knocked around for a couple of days there and then knocked on the gate of the U.S. base and saw it from their side. Right up until April 2004 we were rolling like that.

ANNE GARRELS | **NPR**
The Green Zone is, for intents and purposes, locked—we are locked out of it. I broke the rules and went in with a contractor, and did a tour of the Green Zone, went to some bars and hung out—openly. I did not hide my microphone in this case, and people were not nearly as forthcoming as I might have wished, but nonetheless, I got at least a slightly clearer picture, and was able to at least portray what the Green Zone really is like—this bizarre environment where you've got the CIA compound and the Bechtel compound and this security company compound and then the plush AID [Agency for International Development] compound, and the new sports facility for the military, and the embassy guys live over here, and then the security companies have their own bars. And the drug of choice happens to be steroids in this war. Who'd have thunk it?

III

THE REIGN OF THE COALITION PROVISIONAL AUTHORITY

JON LEE ANDERSON | *THE NEW YORKER*

I returned before the end of June 2003 and stayed for the summer. Of course, this is when the insurgency really did pick up, when Paul Bremer, the CPA [Coalition Provisional Authority] administrator, was getting a grip on his job [the CPA served as a transitional government from April 2003 until June 2004]. And I wrote a long piece in *The New Yorker*, which appeared in August—I think the title was "Iraq's Bloody Summer."

I did have an interview with Paul Bremer on my last night in the country, though I'd already filed my piece. And I came away pretty disheartened by what I saw as a very kind of imperious, closed-off Green Zone under the CPA.

I remember receiving e-mails that I think we all received, announcing civic action—little civic action jobs like "beanies for Baghdad," handing out beanie toys—and all of this sort of bureaucracy that was setting up within the confines of Saddam's old Republican Palace, and a real disconnect with what was going on outside the walls of the Green Zone, or what was then coming to be called the Green Zone. All the Iraqis I knew were going through various degrees of despair and some fled the country that summer; there were the first assassinations taking place, the influx of refugees coming back, the setting up of newspapers, political parties—it was a real Tower of Babel.

PATRICK COCKBURN |
THE INDEPENDENT (LONDON)

At a certain point, in 2003, I remember the exact moment the British had moved inside the Green Zone, and I remember going to see a senior diplomat who I actually knew quite well and who was actually quite intelligent. But because they were inside the Green Zone, they knew less and less about what was happening in Iraq, and what they did know was all second-hand. Now on this day, I was rather late to see this diplomat because there were enormous traffic jams all over Baghdad because there was a shortage of fuel, of gasoline.

So I was talking to him and I mentioned this to him and he said, "But I just looked at figures showing there's plenty of gasoline." Now everybody in the rest of Baghdad knew that there was a shortage of gasoline. The only people that didn't were inside the Green Zone.

ALISSA RUBIN | *LOS ANGELES TIMES*

Well, I always personally found [U.S. government briefings] valuable. I know many other people didn't because if you looked at them in terms of objective truth, they weren't very useful. But in terms of how the U.S. government wanted us to see things, they were quite useful. And it's important to know what the government's narrative is. Because in any conflict there are competing narratives, and our job, from my point of view, is to sort through them and provide a reality check on all of them.

And you know, there were Iraqis you could talk to who would say things are terrible, and obviously things are much more terrible now than they were then, and to some extent people were complaining about things that only seemed terrible because they weren't what they'd expected. There was a great sense of disappointment. That's a different kind of terrible than what people are dealing with now, which is a real, constant fear of bombings, sectarian killings, being forced to move from their homes. Really, the stuff of very serious civil strife and conflict. Similarly, the administration wanted to tell the story of a budding democracy, and there wasn't a budding democracy. There were some elements of it, but there was also a sort of eruption of long suppressed religious feeling and populist politics that was quite uncontrollable and a whole variety of forces that the administration didn't really understand very well. But you have to know what they were trying to tell you in order to see the whole picture, and to see where they were off, and where in fact some of what they were saying might not be so far off.

PATRICK COCKBURN |
THE INDEPENDENT (LONDON)

I went to some CPA briefings. I thought that they were very propagandistic. They were based in trying to prove and make a political point that the U.S. being in Iraq was and is fighting the war on terror. This meant continual emphasis on foreign groups, when there was in fact very little evidence for this. In fact, all the evidence was the other way. The insurgency was almost entirely Iraqi. And there might have been many insurgents who were formerly in the army but it was always presented as if this was somehow orchestrated by former senior officials around Saddam. Again there was no evidence for this. I found it interesting to know what was the official line being put out, but I thought it was the crudest propaganda and not useful in terms of actual objective information.

JON LEE ANDERSON | *THE NEW YORKER*
I remember going to a few of those briefings and seeing—especially in the Bremer period—the kind of almost shout-downs of journalists who dared to suggest that there was anything approaching an insurgency in Iraq. I still remember the date: it was August 7, 2003, and I suggested to Bremer that I wondered how he felt in terms of his access. Now, I said this very diplomatically; after all, he was the senior government official and I was a reporter, and I said in very diplomatic terms: "How do you feel in here, you have these big barriers"—they were erecting even more permanent barriers around the Green Zone—"How do you feel in here? I'm traveling outside and I see that you have to go out with armed escorts. How reliable do you feel your information is about the state of the country and the way people feel?" And he said, "Fine," and I said, "Well, I'm hearing a lot of increasing anger by a lot of

the Iraqis I know, and it has me worried," and it did, and I said, "I wonder what you think about that." And he got very angry with me. He became visibly testy and he said, "I don't know who your sources are. I go all over this country and I don't hear the things you're hearing. I don't know where you get your information." And that was the end of that. I left the country in mid-August 2003, feeling really quite demoralized and upset and worried about what was going to happen in Iraq, because I thought there was a real divide between perception and reality. Speaking for myself, I found the CPA to be very much a kind of an American bureaucracy that almost immediately had isolated itself. And shrewdly, the insurgents, the early insurgents, perceived that as well, and did everything they could to make the occupation of Iraq less a story of gradual reconstruction and pacification and one of counterinsurgency and one of occupation.

BORZOU DARAGAHI | *LOS ANGELES TIMES*
I just remember having this feeling like— this is a very political exercise, and they're a product for the media at this point. What would be really horrible is if the CPA actually believes this crap. And I remember thinking that from the very beginning: I hope they don't believe this stuff, I hope they're not consuming this stuff themselves. And pretty soon it started dawning on me: No, they're not just BSing us because we're the public, they actually believe this stuff. My God, are we in trouble!

L. Paul Bremer arrives at Al-Shaab stadium in Baghdad to congratulate the Iraqi national soccer team after its surprise victory over Saudi Arabia. May 15, 2004. AP Wide World/Saurabh Das

RAJIV CHANDRASEKARAN |
THE WASHINGTON POST

The military was far easier to deal with, and, in some ways, far more understanding of what we were doing than the CPA. Their press office was headed by Dan Senor, Bremer's spokesman. Their press office was packed with Republican Party loyalists, people who were hired for their political views, not because they possessed a great degree of expertise in public relations or expertise in the Middle East or in post-conflict reconstruction. They were the ones who had put people on blacklists—they were just incredibly sensitive about anything that might not project the CPA in the most favorable light possible. Reporters were seen as either sympathetic and on their side or those who didn't get it. And if you didn't get it, either you were perhaps granted some interviews so that you would get it or you would be written off as a lost cause.

PATRICK GRAHAM | FREELANCE WRITER

One really interesting thing was to sit down with people who were either in the insurgency or close to it and watch the [CPA] briefings on Al-Jazeera or Al-Arabiya. I did that a lot, and that was really interesting because what happened was Dan Senor or [Brigadier General Mark] Kimmitt [another of Bremer's spokesmen] would basically insult the insurgency, either by calling them small criminals, or really demonize the Sunni minority.

I think those briefings were one of the reasons that the Sunni minority became so anti-American, because they were aimed for an American domestic audience, and the contempt that Kimmitt and Senor heaped on the Sunnis and the people that were fighting—"dead-enders" and "criminals," "weak and coward-like," and all the insults that he used—really got the back up of the people. Those briefings were key to making the Sunni minority realize that they would not be part of the new Iraq. I think that Senor and Kimmitt were one of the major forces in making the country fall apart. They were very effective in their propaganda for journalists and for Americans who didn't know what was going on, but in Iraq it was a disaster. Even the Shia couldn't believe what they were saying, they were just so dishonest. That was my reaction. The briefings—this may work in New Jersey, but in Iraq it's a disaster.

General [John] Abizaid [the head of U.S. Central Command] went to Fallujah—I think it was Ramadan, it was around November 2003—and his convoy was attacked, and I was sitting watching TV with a group of people who had family members in the insurgency, and the question for Kimmitt was, "Do you think that it was an organized attack?" And he said, "No, no, this was just nothing . . . it's just a group of criminals attacking the"—I can't remember exactly—"this group of criminals in Fallujah who are very unpopular." And the group of people sitting with me were laughing. They thought the insurgency had intelligence that Abizaid was there, that it was a very coordinated attack, the people were very, very pleased by it—it was the exact opposite of the way it was being portrayed. It was actually an example of how strong and well-organized the insurgency was. And Kimmitt's denial of it and his contempt for it was completely misleading to an American audience. And just made the Iraqis that I was with laugh at him.

LUKE BAKER | REUTERS

The people within the U.S. military that dealt with the press in Baghdad were quite intimidating toward us at times. They felt that we asked too many questions when Reuters had people detained, for example, after the incident in Fallujah [in January 2004]. These were Iraqi employees of Reuters, cameraman and soundman and a driver, who were shot at when they were trying to film an incident after a U.S. helicopter had been brought down. And they were filming at the scene; they were shot at by U.S. troops. They then jumped in their car and left because they were worried that they were being fired upon. The U.S. troops chased them down, helicopters chased them down, firing on them, and then detained them. [The military] said that they were basically terrorists posing as journalists at the scene, who fired on U.S. troops—I mean it's absolute fantasyland. But they were detained, held, abused, put in stressful positions, sort of threatened, stripped, made to do obscene things, and eventually they

were released, and that's when we called for an investigation.

But what I was going to say is that when we asked questions about that in press conferences, and I would go to the press conferences in Baghdad, the general that was the main spokesman, General Kimmitt was very dismissive of us, threatened us, asked us not to ask more questions. [Before] one press conference he asked me, "Are you going to ask me any more obnoxious questions?" and I said I might, and he said, "Well, why don't you ask me them now?" I said, "Well I'd rather ask you on the record in the press conference." And he said, "Well," tapping the gun at his side, "You've gotta watch out." Joking, but tapping the gun at his side.

CAROLINE HAWLEY | BBC

We had the most difficulty with the CPA when Paul Bremer was in power. He had given an interview to a BBC program called Panorama that was quite a hard-hitting interview, and I don't think he was used to that. And certainly after that we had a difficult time getting access to Paul Bremer. I understood there were threats that we might be barred from embeds as a result. That actually didn't happen, but there was certainly a kind of air of nastiness, and I had it reported back to me from one coalition official that other coalition officials were accusing me of being able to smell sewage in a bed of roses.

JON LEE ANDERSON | *THE NEW YORKER*

I do fault the CPA and the coalition for having done its best to keep bad news away from the public, and there's been a number of ways they've done that. There is now this notorious writ that no American coffins can be photographed; Bush's decision never to appear at the funeral of a soldier. This, in addition to the daily playing down of bad news, from Bush all the way down to the field command level, over a very crucial period of time, has confused the public, made journalists' jobs much more difficult, and to a certain degree I regard this huge propaganda effort as also pernicious and having been extremely dangerous to us.

Because, for instance, months before people began writing about how dangerous the Baghdad airport highway was, the Americans and the Brits—I'm speaking of the military—stopped using the road. They stopped using the road. They didn't announce it; they choppered to and from the Green Zone. Did they admit openly that that road had become Suicide Alley? There was one particular series of months, I think it was the fall of 2004, in which there had been forty-four suicide bombings along the road, just that little stretch of road.

A few months before Marla [Ruzicka, an aid worker and activist] was killed [April 16, 2005], there was a willfulness about the way Baghdad, the war, Iraq was being presented, the security situation, which I think also led a great number of people to Iraq who were subsequently kidnapped and

killed, who should have known better but didn't, because of the nature of the place [and] the idea that "Oh, only six out of the sixteen provinces are dangerous," that kind of language. I think that this made it very difficult.

ELIZABETH PALMER | CBS NEWS

It was cognitive dissonance to sit in those press briefings, and it became funny, because inevitably there'd be a new reporter at the press briefing of the day who'd—we'd hear the spin and how everything was terrific and they'd repaired water plants and restored power and so on, and then the newcomer would put up his hand and say, "'Scuse me, but what I'm seeing out on the streets has nothing to do with what you're describing and I'm wondering if you could explain the discrepancy" [laughing]. And everybody in the press corps would smile because it really was the fresh eye, the freshly realized, the total disconnect, you know?

PATRICK GRAHAM | FREELANCE WRITER

At one point, I was asked by someone who said he knew I was a Canadian, and he said, "We know you work for the Canadian CIA," and he's a former Iraqi intelligence guy. "No, I don't work for them." And he goes, "I know you do. You get me a job." They just assume, a lot of it was just assumed that you were an intelligence person. I mean after Saddam, the notion of a journalist was crazy. And then when people saw the kind of stuff coming out of Kimmett and Senor on TV translated into Arabic, their view was that anybody associated with them must be working for them, 'cause it became a cultural war.

JAMES HIDER | *THE TIMES* (LONDON)
In Fallujah the Americans had dropped some bombs [in late February 2004], some 500-pound bombs showing the Iraqis that they were still here. I think they call it "dissuasive fire" or something like that. And we went to this little house just outside Fallujah, and we met these people—the bomb had landed fairly close to their house. It hadn't hit anything, it just landed in the desert, and the people said, "Our neighbor, his wife had a miscarriage from the shock of the bomb. What were they bombing? We're innocent people, just peasant farmers." You know, they were very confused about why this bomb had been dropped. Apparently, as far as I could tell, it had been dropped to dissuade the guerrillas from chancing their arms—because they had just attacked a police station a week before or something. So it was a show of force.

And I went back to the Green Zone and [Lieutenant] General [Ricardo] Sanchez [commander of coalition ground forces] was doing a press conference, and I had this completely surreal exchange with him. I said, "I've just been out in Fallujah and you've bombed a field, a woman's had a miscarriage, what were you trying to do?" And he said, "We hit what we were aiming at." And I said, "What were you aiming at?" And he said, "What we hit." And I started

laughing and everyone started laughing at this bizarre exchange, and I think he thought they were laughing with him. But I think they were laughing at this bizarre rhetoric of the Green Zone that had no relation really to what was going on around.

Iraqi women and children watch U.S. paratroopers
in the 1-504th regiment of the Eighty-second
Airborne Division, nicknamed the "Red Devils,"
raid their house in Nassar el al Salaam, a suspected
insurgent compound. November 26, 2003.
Chris Hondros/Getty Images

IV

OMENS AND
INCIDENTS

NIR ROSEN | FREELANCE WRITER

The daily things the Iraqis endure—and those that I experienced just because I looked Iraqi and then because I was a male, and a so-called "male of fighting age." My [new Iraqi] friends would ask me, "Why do Americans say 'fuck' so much, what's this word fuck?" I heard that a few times. "Why do Americans spit so much?" They didn't know about chewing dip—the tobacco thing. So they see Americans spitting all the time; they're going into a house on a raid, and in order to stay awake they chew dip and they're spitting constantly, spitting all over people's yards, things like that. Having to deal with the barbed wire everywhere, the tanks and Humvees blocking traffic in your roads, pointing their guns at you, firing into the air, shouting at you. It was constant humiliation and constant fear, because they control your life. They have these huge guns and you can't even communicate with them adequately. And that summer [2003], it was just unbearably hot and American soldiers were dressed in all that gear. Obviously they were not in a good mood. Iraqis had no electricity. They were in a bad mood. It was always very tense, they were always shouting at Iraqis and shouting at me sometimes. I was walking down the street toward a checkpoint once, and I heard one American soldier say to the other, "That's the biggest fucking Iraqi I ever saw." And the other soldier said, "I don't care how big he is, if he don't stop moving I'm gonna shoot him." And there were one or two other times I heard soldiers talking about shooting me, and whether it was in jest I don't know, but at least I understood and could shout, "Don't shoot, I'm an American!" Most Iraqis couldn't, and that's a very scary thing.

BORZOU DARAGAHI |
LOS ANGELES TIMES

I know how religious the people in Iraq are, how traditional they are with regard to gender relations and stuff like that. I would see certain stuff and I would just cringe and want to say [to U.S. soldiers], "You guys are really, really making a bad name for yourself here by storming into this guy's house with your shoes on. This guy's done nothing and yet you're going to make an enemy out of him because he's gonna talk about you guys for the rest of his life, and that day when they came storming into my house with their shoes on—nobody walks into my house with their shoes on!"

One time I was really tempted to say something to U.S. soldiers when I was in Najaf. And Najaf is a very American-friendly place in general. And there were these soldiers and they were just sitting there, taking pieces of bread and throwing them at each other. They were just kids—like twenty-two years old—just playing around. There's these Iraqi police officers looking at this from out the window and they're just totally aghast. They're totally shocked: Look at what they're doing to bread! You know, bread is considered holy in Islam. You know, you're just not supposed to do that. People pick up pieces of bread and you're not supposed to step on bread. You're not supposed to play with bread. And I felt tempted to say something and I didn't. I just didn't feel it was my place.

GEORGES MALBRUNOT | *LE FIGARO*

I remember I made a report in June [2003], interviewing the people who were dealing with the CPA. And I found that they were going nowhere because they were too inexperienced. And I remember I interviewed the ex-U.S. ambassador who, at this time in June, was responsible for the U.S foreign minister. He told me, "I can't tell you anything," and he came with dirty shoes and he told me, "I'm about to leave, my mission of two months is already over." So I told myself, if the U.S. sends people every two months to rebuild Iraq, they are going straight to the wall. So there was an example that this operation would lead to a failure.

ELIZABETH PALMER | CBS NEWS

I've been struck by how essentially humane a lot of the soldiers are, with a very strong sense of right and wrong, which I think comes with growing up in America. And how ill-equipped they were to apply that to a situation like Iraq, without enough historical or geographical or cultural knowledge to actually—unless they were under the command of a very gifted officer, and there are some who are extremely well-equipped, but a lot of them are not—to apply that sort of fairness to Iraqi society. I feel that a huge majority of them are good men trapped in an impossible situation and have not really understood where they are historically, as well as culturally and physically. I think they're hostages of a terrible situation as well; it's given me enormous sympathy for them, and certainly a new appreciation for how ill-prepared they were for the mission, at least in the early days.

I remember early on in Baghdad—it must have been the end of 2003—some American soldiers who were very keen to befriend a couple of families—families who had been, who were essentially caretakers of properties in Baghdad. They were very poor and these soldiers wanted to befriend the children. They had this tremendous human instinct to try and help them make life easier. It was just at the time when the insurgency was really getting going, and Iraqis who were seen to have relations with the American forces were in great danger, and the soldiers found it very difficult to accept that this gesture of friendship—their wanting to help look after these children and give them gifts and so on—could, in fact, get the family killed.

NIR ROSEN | FREELANCE WRITER

I tried to interact with the Iraqis who were being ignored. And even by then there was a great deal of literature being produced by various religious organizations; they all had their own newspapers and journals and magazines and CDs, and they were very clear about their position and their grievances and their attitude towards the Americans. And I think the Americans, for some reason,

didn't take religion that seriously as a factor in Iraqi society, which is weird because we're like the most religious nation in the industrialized world. We have a born-again Christian president and the religious right is so powerful, but we didn't think that religion was an important motivator for Iraqis. So we just ignored that, except for the so-called moderate clerics who we could try to use to our advantage. But that Iraqi anger and hostility toward the American occupation, and fear of the Americans, and fear that the Americans are going to corrupt their values, steal their women, bring the Jews in to create a greater Israel, bring the Jews in to divide the land—all these fears that just sounded stupid to us were real for them.

LARRY KAPLOW | COX NEWSPAPERS

In April 2003, there was the big Fallujah killing, where members of the Eighty-second Airborne opened fire on a demonstration in Fallujah after they said they had heard shots fired. And they killed anywhere from ten to maybe twenty-five Iraqis there. First of all, we could just drive out there in those days. We heard about it somehow, I think maybe on some radio report, and just drove out to the scene and showed up at this little school in the middle of the Fallujah neighborhood. And the Eighty-second Airborne guys were there. And they said, "Okay, come in, we'll show you around, and we'll tell you our version of what happened." And then you could walk across the street and talk to Iraqis who were around there, and ask them what

Iraqi women watch
as U.S. forces lead
away suspected
insurgents after gun
battles between
insurgents and Iraqi
and U.S. forces
broke out in a Sunni
neighborhood in
Baghdad. July 5,
2004. Chris Hondros/
Getty Images

happened, although it was difficult to get a clear version from either side. It turned out to be a seminal event. Later when you'd talk to insurgents in the days to come, you'd hear them refer to that event.

PATRICK COCKBURN |
THE INDEPENDENT (LONDON)

I was struck at the beginning at how the rules of engagement appeared to allow U.S. forces to open fire when there were civilians around. As in the early stage in Fallujah, according to what has emerged subsequently in writings from there. It was shooting at a crowd of demonstrators in Fallujah which gave the first real boost to militancy there.

LARRY KAPLOW | COX NEWSPAPERS

A U.S. official who was supposed to be the central Iraq administrator for Jay Garner, [U.S. Director of Reconstruction and Humanitarian Assistance in Iraq, March–May 2003], she came in to meet us. She was doing a sort of walkthrough around the palace we were in. They brought her into the room and she let us ask some questions, and people asked about the killing in Fallujah and what she thought had happened, and she had not heard about it. And this was more than twenty-four hours afterwards and I remember at the time, you know the typical way rumors go here, the Iraqis were saying something like ninety people had been killed. It wasn't nearly that many, but I remember Michael Slackman, then of the L.A. *Times*, saying to her, "You haven't heard that the U.S. Army killed ninety people in Fallujah yesterday?" And she said, "No, I haven't heard about it and I guess I should find out why I haven't heard about it."

Well, subsequently, we found out that the reason was because the army wasn't clueing in Garner's people on anything, and they were almost ignoring them. And they also, these people didn't have any equipment, and we were asking them, "How do we call you, so we can find what's going on?" and they would say, "We only have one phone right now and we have to use it for our business, so maybe you can just kind of come to the gate or come to our door." And then eventually they said, "Okay, we can dedicate this phone for media calls for certain hours on certain days."

We were all shaking our heads because like reporters, these people had been basically parked in other countries, mostly in Kuwait, before the war began. And I was able to buy my own Thuraya phone with my company's money before I came in, and so could all of us. So there is a room full of reporters being told by these high ranking officials on this important mission from the American government that they weren't able to get phones in the same way we could. It was just eye opening and a discouraging meeting from the point view of how this is going to go.

We'd been trying to get in touch with these people for days, and trying to figure out how to interface with them, and it turned out there was nothing to interface with. They weren't being clued in on what was happening around the country, and they didn't have any capabilities. It gave us our first clear picture of what kind of planning was done for the administration of Iraq.

RAJIV CHANDRASEKARAN | *THE WASHINGTON POST*

I still recall in Fallujah, [well before the first American offensive there in April 2004], going around with U.S. forces there and accompanying a military commander to a city council meeting. The Iraqis would say just what the commander wanted to hear. The commander would leave. We'd chat outside. He'd think he was making great progress and the Iraqis were on board, the mayor was a partner for peace and development. You go back later that day or the next day and talk to these guys, and it's clear they never believed any of what they said. They were just saying this because they wanted to please the Americans, because they wanted contracts to build schools and roads. Their true allegiances were very different. In fact, the mayor who became a great partner for peace was run out of the city and fled to Syria after charges of corruption and being in cahoots with the bad guys.

I felt that the military was in some ways overly idealistic. They really didn't have the depth of knowledge in terms of who were the good guys, who were the bad guys. What were people's agendas. I dare say, it was tough for anybody to figure this out short of spending really lots of time there. But they would have people who they thought were their trusted allies and partners. But

these were just guys, often, who were trying to steer contracts towards their buddies, who would say to the Americans, these guys are causing trouble, and it was just because they were from a rival tribe or they were competitors in a commercial sense. You had people sidling up to the Americans and in many cases the soldiers would sort of think, "Oh, this guy wears a suit, he speaks English, he'll be my partner here."

ANNE GARRELS | NPR

All the openness that we had enjoyed in those first months became a liability; people knew where we lived and worked, people both in the neighborhood and elsewhere had come to visit us, had come for meals, all of that, and the building was indefensible. So that combination of factors made it imperative that we move, and so then I launched on a search for a house that had security features—that was set back from the street, that had a wall around it, that was anonymous—people wouldn't know where we lived. One of the rules that we instilled was that we wouldn't tell people where we lived. People would not, unless we knew them extremely well, come to the house.

PATRICK GRAHAM | FREELANCE WRITER

The U.S. Army propaganda about who the insurgency was—that they were dead-enders and it was over, a bunch of criminals—was very effective, and that was essentially what was written for a long time. So I think that, in many ways, there was an enormous amount of press self-censorship early on, for about almost the first year of the invasion.

If you look back at how things were reported in that first year, it was pretty close to the way the U.S. government wanted it to be presented, which is, "It's not so bad, it's coming along, we've got a few criminals but we're handling them," when, in fact, what was going on was the Eighty-second Airborne in Fallujah was doing what aggressive, elite units always do, which is create a lot of enemies.

By September or October of 2003, the Eighty-second had already killed at least forty people around Fallujah, probably more like one hundred, some of them even local police, a lot of them kids, all of them from a tribal area. You just knew things were going to go badly.

ALI FADHIL | TRANSLATOR, REPORTER

[In Najaf, August 2004], me and Ivan Watson [of NPR] found ourselves at the top of a tower. We found two American soldiers, very, very young soldiers—they were snipers—at the top room of the tower, and they invited us to eat the MREs [Meals Ready to Eat]. And we were very happy because we didn't eat anything, like only eggs and potatoes all of these days, because there is no food in the city. And we ate with them and started chatting with them, and myself personally, I had like a friendship with them, and one of them called me to come and hold the sniper machine and look through the sniper zoom and look to the [Imam Ali] Shrine, because I wanted to look at it. And we were like joking about the situation until

the moment when suddenly we heard the voice coming from the shrine for the prayers. At that time the two soldiers were back in position. They were furious, and I said, "What's wrong?" They said, "The sound—it means something," and I said, "What?" They said, "It does mean that they're calling their soldiers to come kill us, isn't that right?" I said, "No, it's not. It's prayer calls." It seems like these soldiers didn't know that these are prayer calls, because it's long, long prayer calls—it's prayers they do for the martyrs. And they thought that this was something like a call to start fighting.

PATRICK GRAHAM | FREELANCE WRITER

Iraq wasn't a country that was fact-checkable, right? It wasn't a country where there were a lot of facts. And it wasn't a country that anybody knew anything about, so your problem wasn't selling the story. It was convincing touchy magazines to run things. I had a story on insurgents killed because the magazine couldn't fact-check it [the story eventually appeared in *Harper's*, which had not commissioned it]. American magazines have been beaten up very badly by various scandals, and they just couldn't take a risk. If you said this is a group of insurgents that I'm with, they're not a bunch of former Baathists, they're fighting for kind of tribal, nationalistic reasons—that was the opposite of what was being written in the press in the fall of 2003. The majority of the articles were that they were a group of Baathists, they're dead-enders, they're criminals, they're disgruntled Sunnis who want to take over the country again. The insurgency was over, the insurgency would soon be over. And I was saying, "No, actually, this is an expression of a minority that's scared and doesn't feel that it's going to participate in the future of the country. It's very tribal; it has to do with the cultural context." And it's very hard to prove that.

GHAITH ABDUL-AHAD | *THE GUARDIAN,* GETTY IMAGES

It was a very close call. It was up until that day that I considered myself sort of separated from what [photo] I was shooting, separated by my lens. And I was someone who came into this with this background that I can't see blood, anything that is related to hospitals or blood or death, I really can't see it. My mother died when I was really young; I spent a lot of time with her in the hospital, so I really can't be around these things. But then again, I do war photography.

Early in the morning, the insurgents attacked an armored vehicle and a friend of mine from Getty knocks on my door and says, "There was an attack on Haifa Street, can you go and cover it." This was just like forty minutes later, and I was sure by the time I got there the whole area would be cornered off and I wouldn't get access. It was in September [2004] and I'd spent all of July and August in Najaf covering the fighting there and I hadn't recovered yet. So part of me was really just wishing that the whole area would be cornered off so I could go there and take the pictures, come back—this is how it works.

So we get there, the armored vehicle is on fire, and U.S troops were there. We get to the scene, and I was going to take pictures of the burning armored vehicle. We see two small helicopters, and people started running away, and there was this explosion and people run away. And then later I see the small helicopters and I take pictures and I see the people running away. And I see a group of people, around five, six guys on the ground in the middle of the street. One has lost a leg, bleeding, you can smell the smell of burning flesh, and still at that moment I was separated from the scene, I wasn't conscious of what was happening. And then the helicopters come back, and everyone runs. And then I thought, "Okay, let's run because they're running." And then there was another explosion, and white smoke everywhere, a small piece of shrapnel landed on my forehead. And I felt this hot thing on my head and then I saw blood dripping on my camera.

At that moment, we were five or six taking shelter, and I see three, four guys just in the middle of the street. And they were left I think from the second attack, and they were just left in the street, and they were dying. And one of them kind of pushes himself up, looks around and is looking, looking for something, he looks left, tries, stretches his hand, and falls in the middle of the street. A guy next to me, his leg was almost amputated, and he was bleeding very hard and slumping. And I didn't really want to touch him, he would be okay. Up until that moment, my experiences of people dying in front of me came from movies. And then you believe that someone is hit, or losing a leg, they will be screaming like hell. And everyone is silent. Everyone is silent, no one is screaming. Another guy was crying, weeping, an old man, a big fat guy, was weeping silently. And I remember I was so scared and I was trying to lay flat, but still I would try to stand up, take a couple pictures, and then lie back down again. And I was taking pictures of some guy dying next to me, and still believed that this guy is fine, he's not screaming. He's fine, he's just injured. As this guy is slumping more and more, you know, he's dead, the Palestinian guy bleeding, another Palestinian guy on the phone, screaming for help. And then the helicopters go, people venture into the street. I ventured into the street, I see this little kid lying in the middle of the street, I'm taking pictures, "Oh, he's just sleeping." I don't want to come very close to him, I don't want to wake him up. It's such a mess, and then you realize all the people who you thought were sleeping, who were not screaming, who were fine, they were all dead. And at the end of that day, something like twenty, twenty-two civilians were killed.

Up until this moment I was separated from the scenes of car bombs by my lens: it was something else, it was not reality because I see it through this viewfinder, and all you care about is the light, where it's coming in, the composition, the light. So you are separated. But the smell, the smell is always there. But that day, when you are part of the scene, when you are hiding, all these kids behind this building, and you are trying to take shelter and you are trying to make yourself flat, and you wish that your height is only two inches so you can go flat to the curb. It was that day when this glass wall that was separating me from the scenes of car bombs shattered.

V

ENEMIES AND CIVILIANS

ANNE GARRELS | NPR

I think that in the early months it was seeing the absolute lack of security in the country, and Iraqis feeling increasingly that Americans didn't care about their lives—going into neighborhood after neighborhood where American patrols would go in to do a search, and the searches would go wrong, and the next thing, there would be huge gunfights. And often because of mistakes, errors, lack of understanding— they wouldn't set up checkpoints at either end of the street, so the next thing, an innocent car would drive by.

You know, you saw this again and again: raids that went awry unnecessarily, a complete lack of cultural understanding by the troops. One neighborhood I recall going into so well; and I saw American shell casings literally an inch deep all over the street, and they had not blocked off, as I say, the two sides of the street—they had not followed their own protocols. They had gone to do a raid, and an innocent car—it was the depths of summer and the electricity poles blow [out] from the heat every now and then, and it sounds like a gunshot when it explodes, and the troops turned around and thought they were under attack, and they started shooting. An innocent car was driving by at the same time with a couple and three children, and they were massacred. I came right afterwards, because it happened I knew someone who lived on that street very well. And the car was there and the bloody bodies.

And there was just incident after incident like this, and you saw Iraqis who were fence-sitters at best just turning against the

Americans, and it didn't really matter if you were Shiite or Sunni, and that you just saw as a constant drumbeat. Being shot at ourselves at checkpoints that weren't checkpoints because the soldiers were too frightened to set up a checkpoint because they were afraid of car bombs, so that they would hide in the bushes and just basically shoot at any car that passed. There was no attempt to try to tell the Iraqis why the Americans were there, what they were there for, and in the first year there were no Iraqi security forces, so they were dependent on the Americans. And you didn't know how far or close you could get to an American convoy—the only way you learned was when you got shot, and then you knew that fifty meters was about it, and if you got closer, you got blown up. It was so mismanaged on the ground, it was staggering.

ANTHONY SHADID |
THE WASHINGTON POST

It was before Saddam's capture. I think it was November 2003. I remember I was out in the countryside in Ramadi, and I was working on a story about how the American military was arresting relatives of suspected insurgents as a way of pressuring [them]. And about the repercussions this was having on the fabric of villages there. And it had huge repercussions. It created vendettas that I don't think the American military understood they were creating.

Anyway, as far as reporting, Iraqis were telling me just fantastic stories about abuse that I just kind of shook my head and blew them off. But I remember one guy was being so detailed about this stuff that I think I even wrote it down in my notebook—because it was remarkable and maybe the detail made me think: maybe there is something here. Like all of us, I didn't follow up.

JAMES HIDER | THE TIMES (LONDON)

Everyone I knew from the British press had heard stories of beatings, and fairly severe. People would show us the scars of handcuffs on their hands, whatever, the bruised backs, and I don't think we pursued them nearly as rigorously as we should have. I think it's very difficult to prove who's beaten somebody.

The thing was, it was an extremely violent place, Baghdad. People were getting killed every day, beaten up in the street. I mean I saw somebody being dragged out of his car and stabbed by carjackers. It was really difficult to pin anything down in those months after the war. There was so much, people telling incredible stories. It was very difficult to find out any sort of accountability, responsibility. If you went and spoke to a soldier, he'd say one thing, and if you spoke to the Iraqi police, they'd say another. And it was difficult to get any hard evidence. I think this is a classic case of the power of images, and it came from the Americans themselves in the end. Seymour Hersh wrote a story [in *The New Yorker* in April 2004] that basically came from those [Abu Ghraib] pictures, and that was the first proof that we had. But it was very difficult—

you couldn't get into the camps. People would show you a bruise on their back and say, "American did this." So it was very difficult to come down hard on that story. But I think that also we didn't investigate enough because there was so much stuff happening at the time, that we didn't delve into it enough.

LARRY KAPLOW | COX NEWSPAPERS
Well, I didn't ask people about how they were being treated in Abu Ghraib before the big Abu Ghraib story came out, which is probably the biggest single story of the war since the government fell. And in a way I'm glad I hadn't been approached with those stories; I'm not sure I would have believed them if I had heard them before I'd seen the proof, because it seems so outrageous— American soldiers making prisoners get naked and pile on top of each other and simulate sex acts. But after that happened, yes, I was a lot more on the lookout for those kinds of things.

THANASSIS CAMBANIS |
THE BOSTON GLOBE
I heard stories of torture, abuse, from Iraqis I interviewed, and I didn't dismiss them as exaggerations. As with many other things, I tried to figure out ways to confirm them and was unable to until the photos came out. I didn't doubt that they were true, nor was I convinced they were true, but unlike some of the tall tales I heard, these stories seemed plausible. But one of the decisions you have

to make as a war reporter is how much do you go forward with a print [story] that's not confirmable, and I tended to air on the side of caution.

For example, in the summer of 2003 I interviewed people who said they were insurgents and who described attacking Americans, who described ambushes, and talked to me about what their ideology was and how they didn't support Saddam yet were members of the Baath party and now wanted to join an armed insurgency, and I tried to get these guys to prove to me that they were who they said they were and for various reasons they wouldn't. My instinct was these guys were telling the truth but they would not do or show me things, say photographic evidence of their militant activity, that would prove to me that they were anything other than guys talking over tea about how tough they were. So I didn't run the story. Same with prisoner abuse stories. In fact, in the month before the Abu Ghraib scandal I was working on a story about Abu Ghraib, not about torture and abuse, and I interviewed a lot of prisoners for my story. The story was about the huge number of people who were being arrested and then released without charge—which, I think, at that point was like two-thirds of the people who went through Abu Ghraib were ultimately not charged with anything. And the people who were being released were claiming that this experience was turning them against the United States and towards the insurgency. And while I was talking to

Terror suspects, detained in an early morning raid in Tal Afar, about to be transported to a local detention center. June 7, 2005. Christoph Bangert

people they would tell me about usually vague and unspecified claims, and I said, you know, if you know somebody who was tortured put me in touch with them, I'd love to interview them, and people never actually delivered, so I think that's the way a lot of stories don't get told. These are stories that are missed because they're so hard to pin down.

PATRICK GRAHAM | FREELANCE WRITER
If you went to the hospital in Fallujah in the fall of 2003, they would tell you about bodies coming from Abu Ghraib with signs of torture. And you heard a lot about the torture. The Eighty-second Airborne had a camp called "The Farm"—Iraqis called it "The Farm"—and the Iraqis talked about being arrested and being, you know, all the stuff that Captain [Ian] Fishback talked about [Fishback was a captain in the Eighty-second Airborne who protested to his superiors about the harsh treatment of detainees]. Fishback talks about guys, cooks with baseball bats being pissed off and breaking prisoners' legs, right? And the Iraqis, in Fallujah they were talking about this.

I didn't realize the extent of—I had doubts about it. How do you prove it until you find someone who's been tortured? How do you do it until you see the body? And how do you know that body came from there? All you could do was write an interview with an Iraqi that said this happened, but is that enough? I don't

think that's enough to get published in an American paper.

SCOTT PETERSON |
THE CHRISTIAN SCIENCE MONITOR,
GETTY IMAGES
The moment of Abu Ghraib [the photos of abuses were made public in April 2004] reinforced in [the Iraqi] mind all those rumors, all those prejudices—all those concerns that they weren't certain were true but might have been, they now became very, very real. And whether they were real or not, the fact that they were real in Abu Ghraib— that those kind of abuses and those kind of events took place—all of a sudden made, in many Iraqi minds, every single abuse a real thing.

THOMAS DWORZAK | MAGNUM PHOTO
Ask the Pentagon, or ask the military: What harm has photography brought to the effort in the war? In a way, in a sick way, we're pretty corrupted, by the reality—the bad pictures have been taken by their own people. The shocking pictures have been taken by [U.S. Army specialist] Lynndie England. She should get the Pulitzer for investigating. That's what brought out the real dirt. It wasn't us, trying to get in while they rough up some Iraqi a little bit. The big iconic pictures questioning the effort in the war on terror, or whatever they call it—these have been taken by their own people. It doesn't need a professional photographer to take a halfway decent picture. The

pictures in Abu Ghraib, some of them photographically are very good pictures. No photographer has managed to take a more harmful picture—no professional photographer—has managed to take a more harmful picture than these guys in Abu Ghraib.

DEXTER FILKINS | *THE NEW YORK TIMES*
I'll tell you a very good example of a problem that I've had—that everybody's had—with the military, which has never been resolved. The military complains when there'll be an engagement of one sort or another, whether it's a car bombing or whether it's a bunch of insurgents attacking American soldiers or they blow up a Humvee or something. And the headline says, four Americans killed in Humvee attack. And whoever of the American soldiers or civilians or whoever will say, "All you do is report the Americans who were killed and we wiped out those insurgents that day." But, by and large, when you ask them, "Did you return fire and if you did what were the results of that?" they won't tell you, and they'll say, "Well, we don't do body counts." It's a leftover from Vietnam, kind of a bad memory. "We don't do body counts, and so we're not going to tell you how many people we killed and wounded." And that becomes a huge problem because there'll be, say, a large incident, a lot of people have been killed—insurgents, civilians, and American soldiers—huge battles going on, and you're trying to get some sense of what actually happened and

maybe somebody's making an accusation, and they'll say, "Well, we don't do body counts," and that's like just a conversation stopper: "We don't do body counts, sorry." Well, it turns out they really do do body counts, and they always do them. The military will decide that it is in its interests on this particular day to tell you how many insurgents they killed and wounded, they will have a very precise number, and they'll say, "Well, actually, we killed seventeen and wounded forty-two and we took ten of them prisoner." And then you'll scratch your head and say, "Well, I thought you didn't do body counts?"

NANCY YOUSSEF | **KNIGHT RIDDER (McCLATCHY)**
You know, my focus since I've been reporting here has been on civilian casualties. Really since the beginning, actually. In 2003, you know, there were a million stories to pursue. I drove in the day after the regime fell. And there were these dead bodies all over the street, these swollen bodies on the sides of the streets, and I was curious. How many people died, how many civilians died in this conflict? You could go anywhere and you could do anything, and I really wanted us—and Knight Ridder wanted us—to be out on the forefront on civilian casualties. So my three colleagues and I, we got a list of every major hospital—I think it was twenty-one in Baghdad at the time—and we went through and we asked them, "How many civilians died here? How many civilians came in?"

It just seemed natural. It was always about hearts and minds, hearts and minds, hearts and minds, and you would talk to civilians, and they would say, "Well, how can they win our hearts and minds? They're killing us. They're killing us at checkpoints, they're killing us in our houses. What hearts and minds are they talking about?"

To me, if we're going to talk about winning hearts and minds, it begins and ends with how many civilians are being killed in the conflict. It just kept manifesting itself in different ways: Iraqi frustration with U.S. presence here, the growth of the insurgency, the growth of terrorism, the development of al Qaeda—there was always a link back to civilian casualties. And then I thought, as an Arabic speaker and someone who can get out a little bit more, that it was a good use of my resources to focus on that, because we could get to that story in a way that most people couldn't.

It was just on a whim one day. I thought that I'd just go to the Ministry of Health and see if they have the statistics. Because the U.S., at the time, said they didn't have them. I thought, "Who knows, maybe they're keeping them." And the officials there, they gave us the numbers. I said, "I don't suppose you have, you know, the number of civilians killed. I don't suppose you have this divided by coalition versus noncoalition." They said, "Sure!" And they handed me the sheet, and I thought, "Well, good Lord."

That was in September of 2004. And one thing to point out: at the time, Iraq was

pretty well known for its record-keeping. You know, there are some countries where you can't depend on records at all. But there was a real, I don't know, commitment to details, and to records, and to being accurate in the record-keeping. So I felt really comfortable going with their numbers. The Iraqi Health Ministry is sort of an objective group that has no incentive to taint the numbers one way or the other at the time. I mean these were statisticians, they weren't politicians. So, I felt it was important to import [into an article on civilian casualties published on September 24, 2004] what they had recorded, based on their information. They weren't doing it haphazardly.

I wanted to keep following it, but I've gone back, oh, maybe four or five times since, and they will not release numbers on their records of Iraqis killed by coalition forces. And no one else has ever reported that number. There've been reports of civilians killed, but never that breakdown. Well, [the official at the Health Ministry] hinted at why. He said, "I'm not allowed to release them. I got in trouble, it caused a lot of problems, it went all the way up to the Health Ministry. You know, the top levels of the government went crazy and were upset about these numbers being released."

HANNAH ALLAM | KNIGHT RIDDER (MCCLATCHY)

We haven't been aggressive enough in having our home bases petition the Pentagon and the administration to reveal these [civilian casualty] figures. They keep them, we know they keep them and we have some partial figures released from time to time or somebody's been leaked something. But I think it's shameful that they have the figures and won't release them.

And I just don't understand why. I'm a firm believer in "the key to PR is honesty, honesty, honesty," so why not say, "Look, here they are. War is bloody. There's going to be civilian casualties. Here's what they are. We'll give it to you month to month." And then it wouldn't be this big scary unknown, where you have all these wild speculations that range from hundreds of thousands to a few thousand. And, I think even what they have is not a complete picture, but at least it would be a starting point. And I think it would work to [the military's] advantage because it would be far smaller than some of these estimates that have been put out there.

ALI FADHIL | TRANSLATOR, REPORTER

Me and Ivan Watson [of NPR], we were walking the streets, we actually walked deep, deep into [Najaf, in August 2004,] where we were trapped with a few people who, it seems, were trapped there for weeks with no water and no food. That was really the moment where we felt bad, me and Ivan. Ivan, he's Russian in origin, he's American Russian—his father lived during the [Second] World War, I think in Europe, in Russia somewhere, and when he was walking and he saw the destruction in Najaf, I remember he told me this, which I couldn't

forget: "Who's gonna compensate all these houses? These are antiques." And he was looking at the electricity wiring and he said, "It's just like what my father was telling me about the world war. It's just exactly how he was telling me. I see the same thing."

As he finished that, we had to go into a side door, because we were hearing these bullet shots coming near to us. It's not the usual sound of a gun, like [makes "Ta" sound], no it's not this. This is the sound of a bullet coming near to you, that sshhhhhhhh—this is, there are bullets coming near to you. And we immediately went to the right, to a very small road, which is a characteristic of this very old city, very antique city, and it's like this house is built—two-story houses, and they were very close to each other and sometimes they were attached, and the yard is one meter, one meter and a half, and we went inside and we found the mother screaming and screaming, and it seems that she was screaming because of the bullet shots we just heard. The bullet shots killed her son, her fourteen-year-old son.

And she was shouting at Ivan, she was telling him, "We are Shiites," 'cause Ivan looks like an American, even though he didn't say that he's an American, but he's a foreigner so he's an American foreigner, and she was shouting. We went inside her house, me and Ivan were pointing the mikes at her mouth, and she was shouting at Ivan. At one time she was holding his vest, shaking him and saying, "Why, why? We love Americans.

We supported you, why you did this to me? Why have you killed my son? My son was the first among his class, my son was supposed to go to medical school! Why have you killed him?" And as she was shouting, we cried, both of us, we cried. It was horrible for us because we felt like it's because of us he was killed, maybe because of us, and even Ivan said that her son was killed because of us, maybe because they saw us go by—anyway.

Her son was very brave. He was angry that his mother and his sisters were thirsty. They didn't have water, they have only very dirty water coming from the pipe. They're sucking at the water to come out, and it was very hot and they needed to cool down, so he went to bring some ice from outside, and when he walked outside into his street, where he used to play, as she said, he died with a bullet in his head, his forehead.

We asked the families if there are other people, and they said yes, there are too many people inside, trapped, and they don't know their situation. And what we did is, Ivan was very angry with the situation and he didn't know what to do, but when we went back to the house—which is not far away, it's only a few blocks—that we used to live in, he found a guy with a cart driven by a mule, and he was selling ice. This crazy guy, we don't know how he thought of selling ice in this place—it might be he was doing something else. But anyway, we asked him, "We're gonna give you money if he can get this ice inside the place where the people are trapped," and Ivan said, "I can pay him whatever he asks," and I asked him how much money he wanted. He

asked for very little money in Iraqi dinars. I said, "No, we're gonna give you twenty dollars," and we gave him twenty dollars. Ivan gave him, actually, twenty dollars, and just for the sake of knowing that the ice goes to the people, I went with him until one of the roads, which is one block from them, and I was watching him giving the ice to these people who were very, very happy. They were waving. "Thanks, thank you," from far away they're shouting. And we were very, very angry, me and Ivan, that day.

PATRICK COCKBURN | *THE INDEPENDENT* (LONDON)

Iraqis don't keep their money in banks because after the invasion of Kuwait, Saddam closed the banks, and when they reopened, people found that instead of the dinar being, whatever it was, one to three dollars to the dinar, that they were getting two thousand dinars to the dollar. After that they generally kept their money at home, and in hundred dollar bills. So often Iraqi houses have a surprising amount of cash in them, but this is the total savings of an extended family. Like anywhere else in the world where people keep large sums of money in their house, they are afraid of someone stealing it.

So if you knock on their door at two in the morning, they're likely to answer it, and they're all armed with guns. The U.S. military didn't seem to realize this, so when the door was answered by an Iraqi with a gun, he was often shot dead—totally innocent farmers or businessmen or whatever. This created an enormous outrage at the time.

LARRY KAPLOW I COX NEWSPAPERS

A country doesn't want to believe that an army they sent overseas, their brothers and sons and fathers, have done bad things. It's very hard to get the home country to accept that fact. And that's not just in America. You see this in other places that have sent armies places. Every time there is a war, a nation goes in here with the whole mythology, and the whole rationale. It's very difficult to work in anything that contradicts the mythology.

COLONEL WILLIAM DARLEY I
MILITARY REVIEW

We have never recovered from the Abu Ghraib thing. And it's likely all the time we're in Iraq, we never will. It will take a decade and beyond. I mean, those pictures, a hundred years from now, when the history of the Middle East is written, those things will be part and parcel of whatever textbook that Iraqis and Syrians and others are writing about the West. Those pictures. It's part of the permanent record. It's like that guy in Vietnam that got his head shot. It's just a permanent part of the history. That will never go away.

HANNAH ALLAM I KNIGHT RIDDER (McCLATCHY)

I was where, out at—was it Abu Ghraib or Buka [a detainee facility in southeastern Iraq]? I can't remember, but it a was U.S.-run detention center, and I had asked for a long time to go into the—I don't remember if they go up or down, it was either level one or level four, but basically the compound

with the most dangerous inmates in the entire U.S.-run detention system. I wanted to see where they were kept, and to see detention conditions and things like that. And so they had let me watch interrogations at Abu Ghraib and were really, really accommodating to me at the prisons. So I go, and finally I get a call from the PAO at the prison that says, "Hey I got good news, you're going to go to the maximum security compound." And I was really excited and we get out there.

And just as we get out there, there's an inmate going absolutely nuts, spitting on everybody. So they put him into this Hannibal Lecter kind of device. And it looked really awful and it took like six people to strap him down. He was spitting, he was going crazy. And they strapped him into this thing that really looked like some medieval torture device. And so I whip out my camera because they told me as long as the photos don't show faces of the detainees I can take whatever picture I want. Which was great. So I was taking a picture, because the inmate's face was covered by a mask, and the PAO said, "Don't. You. Dare." I said, "What are you talking about?" and we had a huge fight right there in front of the guy getting wrestled into this thing. And I said, "Okay, fine. I'm just going to say here they are shoving this guy, six people on one, into this thing, that it looks like he's going to be drawn and quartered. Come on, just let me show it and it takes away the mystery of it." "No, No, No, No," they said. "It will go all over. The Arab press is going pick it up and

A marine guards a detainee
in a makeshift holding
cell in the Iraqi town of
Saqlawiyah. January 20,
2006. Toby Morris

say, 'Look, torture is still going on in Abu Ghraib'" or wherever we were. Camp Buka.

So we had this fight about it, and in the end I didn't take a picture and I just joked about it. I did describe it in as much detail as I could in my piece, but he didn't let me take a picture. Because he was worried that—he said, "I don't doubt your intentions and that I would go with a story that explains this guy was extremely volatile and that he was doing this and this is the only way we could control him." He said, "I don't doubt your intentions, but what I don't want is for the wire services to pick up this photo and the next thing we know it's on Arabiya, Al Jazeera, everywhere else and showing the medieval sort of tactics of the U.S. military on the Iraqis." So I can even kind of see it.

PETER MAASS |
THE NEW YORK TIMES MAGAZINE

I went to Baghdad to do a story about the training of Iraqi security forces. This was February–March 2005, and clearly the moment when the U.S. effort to solve the problem of the counterinsurgency on their own was not working, and they were clearly going to be trying to hand it over to an Iraqi force that hadn't been created yet. One of the units that I had heard about was the special police commandos, which were run by the Interior Ministry. They were not run by the Iraqi Army.

So I get there, and I had already been in touch with a special forces colonel who was advising the Iraqi commandos, and a retired special forces colonel who was also advising them. This special forces colonel tells me that the next day he's going to Samarra because there's a meeting with General Adnan Thabit, the head of the commandoes, and he says, "If you want to come along you can come along." At this point, very few journalists were going on roads outside of Baghdad, even with the American military. It was all on helicopters. These special forces guys, they barrel along roads like that all the time. But journalists hadn't been doing that with them.

We get up to Samarra and there's American military up there, and during this meeting, an American captain who's working with the commandos in Samarra shows up at this meeting. And I start talking to him, he's like a twenty-five-year-old guy, West Point graduate, and he's a really nice guy and we just talk for fifteen minutes, but it was a good talk. And because he's working with the commandos, I say okay, this is it: "Can I embed with you guys? Would you guys like that?" And I talked to his major and his major says, "Yeah, we get no attention for what we're doing up here. We'd be glad to have you." I knew, because I had been up in Samarra and had been talking to that captain, that there was an offensive being planned by the Iraqi police commandos to flush out Samarra for like the third time in three years, and I had to pretend that I didn't even know there was an offensive that was going to be happening there, because that was classified information.

And so me and my photographer Gilles Peress went there. While we were there, they tried to kick me out, because they were nervous. I found out once I got there that, among the many people who weren't comfortable with me being there, was actually the colonel who was in charge of the area. Not just of Samarra but of the broader area. And I went out on this raid where the Iraqi captain or major raised a weapon at a prisoner and threatened to execute him. And word got back to the higher American command that I, *New York Times* journalist, had been present at a threatened execution of a prisoner. And basically all of a sudden my escort—they had sent a major down from Tikrit to be my escort—he came up to me. He had been at my side the whole time and going out on all the patrols with me and all that. And he was okay. He came up to me and just had an ashen look on his face, and he said, "Peter, I just got an order. You've got to be out of here in an hour. There's a convoy leaving and you've got to be out of here." And this was after I'd been there for two days, two or three days. And I said, "I'm not scheduled to leave here for another day or two and I want to stay longer." And he said, "There is no way to appeal this. This is coming down from higher."

So I immediately get on my Thuraya and I call up everybody I know in Baghdad. I mean, the Interior Ministry, and General Petraeus's office. I called the spokesman for General Taluto, who's the commander in Tikrit responsible for the entire northern area. And I say to all these people, "I'm being kicked out of here. I have done nothing wrong. I don't even know why I'm being kicked out. I'm being given no explanation whatsoever. If you people follow through on this, disembedding a *New York Times* correspondent, you know, we're going to be taking it up, I'm going to be taking it up in every venue that I can and it's not going to look good." I knew why they were kicking me out, but because I hadn't been given a reason, I didn't want to announce it. So I just played dumb, you know, "I've done nothing wrong," which is true, "And you're kicking me out." General Taluto—this is the general of the Forty-second Infantry Division, which is a New York State National Guard force—apparently as far as I can tell intervened and said, "No, you're not going to kick *The New York Times* out of Samarra." And so, I had packed my backpack, Gilles had packed his backpack, we had said our goodbyes, you know, and I was just like "Shit," I had made the calls and nothing happened. We're about to get on the convoy when the major who's my escort comes up to me and says, "You can stay."

So I was able to stay, and it was actually a nasty place. There were a lot of nasty things going on there in terms of these commandos being very brutal. There was a detention center there where some very nasty stuff was going on. It was really interesting: they had told me, "You cannot visit the detention center." And I had been told by somebody that they didn't even want me on the street that the detention center was located on. But unfortunately, the detention center was located on the same street as the administration building where all the military planning and meetings were happening. So they couldn't keep me off of it and they knew that. It was a school building, set back about fifty meters from the road. And it was clear that if I expressed interest in going there, if I kind of loitered around there, they would get suspicious and that would make my life more difficult in terms of keeping the access I had. And so I kind of was like, "Oh, no problem, I'm just here to hang out with commandos." And so I expressed no interest in it, didn't push it, because I knew if I pushed it, this is an incredibly sensitive point and I would probably get disembedded again. And what I did was, as discreetly as possible, find out as much as I could, try to talk to some of the soldiers there about it, observe the activity, who was going in, who was going out, what condition they were in, things of that sort.

But the—this was kind of a breakthrough and a mistake that people who were dealing with me made: There was a Saudi who was arrested, they caught, and he was at the detention center. And for whatever reasons, obviously their own propaganda reasons, they decided that it would be good to make this Saudi available to talk to me. So one of the Americans said, "Hey, the Iraqis just captured yesterday this young Saudi, an eighteen-year-old kind, foreign fighter, do you want to talk to him?" And that's a weird kind of offer anyways—interviewing prisoners under the observation of military authorities. It's very strange ethical ground

and very uncomfortable. But I decided, "Okay. I'll do it."

And to my surprise, this American advisor said "Do you want to do this?" and took me over to the detention center, set back fifty meters from the road. We go past the main gate. We go to the detention center. Takes me to an office to the side of it. But basically I'm not able to go into the building, so I can't really see what's going on there. But, you know, I see people being slapped around. I hear people screaming. I see blood on walls. And I'm pretending not to pay attention to that. Because I know that, much as I want to, just tactically, I decided if I show any interest, they're going to take me away. I'm not even taking notes, like "There's blood on the wall." I'm just observing and registering without appearing to show much interest. So I interview the Saudi, and behind me there's a window and there are prisoners behind the window and I hear them vomiting and screaming, and the American advisor who's in this room talking to the Saudi hears the people screaming, leaves the room. I don't know why but I assume to tell the Iraqis, "Hey, keep it down," because when the American comes back two minutes later the screaming stopped.

And when I was hanging out outside, not at that moment this was later, on the street, I hear a gunshot from behind the detention center. And there weren't, there weren't a lot of gunshots there. It was quiet in the center. I kind of raised my eyebrows. It could be an incidental discharge of a weapon that happened, Iraqis are notorious for that. You

know, cleaning their weapon and it fires.
Americans don't do that. Iraqis do. But then,
five minutes later, there's another gunshot
from the exact same location behind the
detention center. And I just, saw it—there
was stuff going on there. And at that time,
this was February–March 2005, although
Abu Ghraib has already happened, this issue
of Iraqi violations had really not been raised
that much, because Iraqi security forces
really didn't exist in significant numbers or
they weren't doing that much, but this was,
this was what they were doing at the time.
And some of that has since come out. I wrote
about it in my story.

Chaos and destruction after a car bomb
explodes at the Imam Ali Mosque during
Friday prayers in Najaf, killing at least
eighty-five people, including one of Iraq's
most important Shiite clerics, Ayatollah
Mohammed Baqir al-Hakim, sixty-four,
who had just delivered a sermon calling
for Iraqi unity. August 29, 2003.
Kate Brooks/Polaris

VI

TURNING POINTS

DEXTER FILKINS | *THE NEW YORK TIMES*
I remember the whole period from October, November, December 2003, everybody—all the reporters—were still playing by the old rules and going where we wanted to go. And everybody would come back more and more and say, "My God, I had something really scary happen today: 'my car got raked by gunfire,' or 'a crowd chased me down,' or 'some guys with masks chased me in a car,'" and so it was clear that the environment was changing, and so we had to respond to that and it took a long time to kind of figure out how to do that.

**RAJIV CHANDRASEKARAN |
*THE WASHINGTON POST***
In early December of 2003, I was driving back from Hillah. A translator, a driver, and I had gone down to do a story on the provincial council there. Each province had its own government council. We talked to the members. On the drive back to Baghdad, we were about half way there and saw what we thought was a big car accident. One of the vehicles was on fire. We saw a couple of bodies on the road. As we're driving by, something caught my eye. I thought, "This is very unusual." Because people were celebrating, were cheering, were very boisterous. I thought, "This is not an accident. This is very strange." So I directed my driver to pull over and my translator and I got out. I kept my notebook in my pocket, and since I'm of a darker complexion, if I don't open my mouth, I'm often mistaken for a dark-skinned guy from Basra. So I just sort of walked through the crowd with my

translator. It became clear that those were Spanish intelligence agents and seven of them had been ambushed on their way down to Hillah. Their bodies were sprawled out on the road and they were being mutilated by this mob. We just stumbled upon them.

ANDREW LEE BUTTERS | FREELANCE WRITER

I could feel things change in February of 2004, although I was slow to pick up on it somewhat. I remember catching a ride back from a dinner in a taxi with Jon Lee Anderson of *The New Yorker*, and someone asked me how things were going, and I said something about safety, "Ah, it's fine, you can do anything." And Jon Lee Anderson said, "I've never been in a society where something so clearly was on the brink of happening." And I was like, "What's he talking about it?" Sure enough, and not very long afterwards, there were the two uprisings in Fallujah and Ramadi. In some ways you feel like a frog, the proverbial frog in boiling water. The changes are so gradual you don't notice it until suddenly things get really bad.

LUKE BAKER | REUTERS

For Ashura [a Shiite holy day], in March 2004, there probably were about a million people estimated gathered in Karbala. It had gone off pretty smoothly—they'd really feared, the government and the military, everyone feared violence. It was the first time that Shiites had celebrated Ashura publicly in Iraq for something like thirty years. On the final day, when the streets of Karbala were the most packed, there was a series of bombings. We were on the streets of Karbala; one bomb went off reasonably close to where we were. Perhaps foolishly we went to it, thinking it was a one-off thing. We were rushing to the site where the bomb had gone off, and another suicide bomber blew himself up between where that bomb had gone off and where we were, probably about thirty feet in front of me, and it just mowed down everyone between me and him. Thirty people were just wiped out in front of myself and the cameraman—a really devastating scene. Then we turned and another bomb went off to our left, doing exactly the same thing to people to our left, and then another bomb went off. I was on the satellite phone trying to call in what was happening, and people then thought that—I was the only foreigner there—I was somehow setting these things off through the satellite phone. They wanted to attack me, but we managed to basically get out of immediate danger.

ALISSA RUBIN | *LOS ANGELES TIMES*

[In March 2004], people in Fallujah had been laying IEDs [improvised explosive devices], and we knew that a serious assault was coming. We had someone with the marines, writing about the marines, and some civilians in Fallujah were killed, and so I felt that we needed to tell the story also from the point of view of the civilian Fallujans. So I went out there to talk to them. And I was in a hospital and a relative of someone who had just been killed came in and he was very angry that there was a foreigner there, although I was properly dressed in an abaya and a hijab, but he became furious and he pulled out a gun. An Iraqi translator I was working with was there and [the angry man] basically held the gun far closer to his head or my head than either of us ever want to see again.

And Suhail [Rubin's translator] told him, "Calm down, stop it. We didn't mean any harm." That sort of thing. And he told him that we were trying to explain what had happened to his relative who had been killed. No one offered to help us or pull the man away, and we walked out of the hospital and survived. Although we were very afraid as we walked out that we'd be shot in the back.

RAJIV CHANDRASEKARAN | *THE WASHINGTON POST*

I spent more than two weeks with the U.S. Marines in Fallujah in April 2004 during the first marine incursion into Fallujah, the one that would eventually result in the marines pulling out and then bringing back a bunch of former Baathist officers called the Fallujah Brigade, which turned out to be a disaster. This was in the spring of 2004.

I was with a marine battalion in the city. We were camped out in an abandoned soda pop factory. We went out on patrol with these guys. We ate the MREs with them. We were taking incoming fire in the evenings with them. We were in the same degree of danger as them. I was just blown away by how a bunch of eighteen-, nineteen-, twenty-year-old kids, from often very broken homes,

inner cities, you name it, how they had come together and were exhibiting what I felt to be very great discipline. We all know there are exceptions to this, but by and large I was just really impressed by their ability to exercise restraint, to have such a disciplined chain of command. The marines would have to go back in again with greater numbers and greater force in the fall of 2004.

ALI FADHIL | TRANSLATOR, REPORTER

The first time I entered Fallujah it was with a Canadian journalist. We went inside Fallujah in April 2004, just a few days after they lynched the four men, contractors. We went to investigate about a recent American riot in a neighborhood called Al-Askari, and the Canadian journalist—his name is Patrick Graham—and I went inside. We found a young man, his name is Yusif. This Yusif lost his brother, because his brother was standing outside his house and the American forces raided there, and they didn't know that the American forces are in the area; what happened, he was holding his daughter, standing outside the house, just in front of the house, and they shot him, a sniper shot him dead by bullet in his neck.

And we arrived at the house—it was a furious moment—people were very angry about the Americans. And of course any foreigner in Iraq is regarded as American, whether he's French or anybody—when they see a face there, you're American until proven otherwise. So they were angry, and we had to deal with them, with their anger, and Patrick was asking questions really, really hard to translate. When he, for example, asked the question, "Was your brother an insurgent?" I replied to him, "I can't translate this—we'll be killed, both of us. Now, I will make it another, a different way."

And he says, "Of course, sure, do what you want—it's dangerous," so the way I translated is—it's the same, but it's kind of a polite way: "We hear that in an American press conference today," of course, we lie about it actually sometimes, "Americans said they killed insurgents, and the Americans said that your brother is one of the insurgents. What do you want to say about this?" So it's kind of polite, and it might be different from how a journalist should approach it, but it's the only way to ask this question. The answer will be different, of course, if you ask it in the first way and then in the second way, but it might kill you, and there is no story in the world worth dying for.

Of course, [Yusif] was angry about the whole question, even though it was polite, and he's not an insurgent, and he said "Come on, I'll prove to you." And the only proof he had was his brother's daughter, who was telling about her dad. He was holding her, and that's it.

RICHARD ENGEL | NBC NEWS

April 2004—things just snapped. It was that period of time. The insurgency, the kidnappings, and the degree of opportunism took off. People became targets. Any westerners became targets. Convoys became targets, contractors became targets, journalists became targets—in a week the insurgency took off and started grabbing people for money. Kidnappings are mostly a money-raising activity; the reason they do it is they want to fund the insurgency or fund themselves. So, they learned: okay, we're going to need, we're going to have this fight, we're going to need to pay for it, and that's when it happened. Things became suddenly very dangerous. And everyone was very exposed because we had had a year, literally one year—April to April—of roaming around the country at our will. There were reporters everywhere, just floating around the country.

And I think maybe that we were a little more realistic about the security situation from the beginning than print continued to be. We had armored cars and escorts even when things were good. Print took the low-profile approach. It operates on a false assumption: that you can be invisible and that people in the Arab world won't know your movements. It's not the case. I lived in Cairo; I couldn't open my window without people wondering, "Oh, why is he opening his window today?" Think of some Italian neighborhood in Brooklyn where everyone knows everyone's business. The Arab world is very much like that.

ANTHONY SHADID |
THE WASHINGTON POST

I think after April 2004, it changed pretty dramatically in all respects. I remember pretty vividly that moment of standing in the street when there was a militiaman manning a checkpoint, wearing a bandolier of bullets, and on a street over there was either a Bradley or a tank, and you got that sense of the street fighting that was talked so much about before the invasion was actually happening at that point.

I had done a story back in 2003 on the village called Thuluyah and I'd gone there quite a few times in 2003. I'd ended up doing a story on a father who'd been forced to kill his son for being an informer for the Americans. And it felt pretty relaxed in 2003 doing those stories. I met the people who had forced the father to kill his son and I met the father himself. I moved pretty casually through the village. And as you move through these villages, you look for people who know everything. You look for the barber, the pharmacist, the people who talk to everybody. I latched on to those people early on, I latched on to the pharmacist, and he really made it easy, getting around the village, talking to people.

[In 2005] I wanted to go back because I was trying to do a story on what life with the insurgents, you know, what life in liberated Iraq was like. I thought this would be a good village because it very much was off limits at this point. The Americans just didn't go in there and, when they did, there was fighting. And I spent three days in Balad, trying to set up some sort of guarantee.

I had met some doctors at the hospital in Balad from this town, on another trip a couple of months earlier. And they had said at that time that they thought they could get me into this village. And so I went and talked to them. On the first day, they said, "Let us make some more calls." And I went

the second day—it's not that safe of a drive from Baghdad to Balad—and they said, "You know, give us one more day." And on the third day I went back, and two of the doctors said they couldn't guarantee my security and the third doctor said he could.

And I thought about it, and I thought, if I were ten years younger and desperate for the story I would have done it. But you think, two out of three isn't great odds. It just kind of hit me that this is an important story, and it's a story about where Iraq is headed and where it's been. And it just wasn't possible.

DEXTER FILKINS | *THE NEW YORK TIMES*
The big turning point was April 2004, when the contractors were killed in Fallujah. I was there about a day before it happened. It was like riding on your horse into a really bad town in a Saturday afternoon Western, you know? And all the shutters were closed, and it was really, really quiet, and you kind of see people peeking out, and…it was really, really tense. And I remember that day because the four contractors who were killed were driving around in exactly the same car that we had, which is a red Pajero. And we had a red Pajero, and so we were driving around, and I remember driving right down the main street, and there was a place where we used to go to eat lunch pretty regularly, a place called Haji Hussein's Kebab House, which I think the Americans took out later that year, they put a JDAM [a guided air-to-surface weapon] through the thing. And it's ironic…it may or may not have been used for whatever, insurgent activity, but it was owned

by Kurds, who are generally quite friendly.

But I remember that day, we went into Haji Hussein's, and it was just like the Saturday afternoon western, and the sheriff walks into the bar and all the voices just drop, and man—I was not wanted there, you know? And we sat down and ate anyway, and I think it was the next day or maybe two days, because I'd left the country the next day I think. So things had been changing pretty rapidly there, particularly in Fallujah, which was always bad, but all over the Suni triangle. So you had the uprising in Fallujah; we had a person kidnapped, two people kidnapped— really, really bad situation—and then you had the Shiite uprising, Muqtada's uprising at pretty much the same time, and we had another two people kidnapped, I mean Burns—John Burns and Shawn Baldwin—a photographer—were blindfolded and taken by the Mahdi Army at night and taken outside of town and told to get out of the car and walk into the field and you can imagine how terrifying that was. Somehow they managed to get out.

So after that—that was the big moment, that was like two years ago—is really when the wall came down, when everybody who didn't have them, for the most part, got guards, stopped traveling outside of Baghdad for the most part, and generally speaking, had to be very controlled in their movements when, you know, the whole Sunni Triangle was essentially written off, and much of the south too, because it's an unfortunate fact of geography that to get into the south, which is relatively safe—relatively—you have to go

through some really awful area to get there; some Sunni towns that are horrible. And it was this kind of Mad Max, horrible scene driving down there—burning cars. When you drive through Mahmudiyah, which is a really, really bad town—Sunni town—the streets are very, very narrow. You have to go through the main street and the bazaar really comes out almost to your car windows, and so people literally can just kind of lean their heads over and look right into your car. And the traffic is horrible so you end up getting stuck in traffic on a very narrow street in the middle of a very crowded bazaar. So if you look like I do, you know, that's not a good thing, so that day, when I went down to Najaf, I ended up staying down there for about two weeks…I lay down in the back seat; I covered myself completely as we went through these towns—it was about an hour or two. We put screens—these black screens up in the windows.

NIR ROSEN | FREELANCE WRITER
The initial proposal [for an article Rosen wrote in May 2004 for *The New Yorker*] was much crazier: they wanted me to get embedded with the resistance. And then once I got to Iraq, they decided that it was politically untolerable for an American to be with people who are attempting to or succeeding at attacking or killing Americans. That wouldn't look good, so they changed it. But it was sort of a suicide mission one way or the other because their guy said it was too dangerous to work there anymore: Jon Lee Anderson wasn't willing to because

he said it was too difficult or too dangerous. So they didn't have anybody, and Sy Hersh recommended that they go with me. And it wasn't much of a risk for them; they gave me five thousand dollars for expenses and sent me over there.

It was very easy—I just took a taxi to Fallujah and hung out with people. A couple different people: one was an Iraqi girl who sometimes worked as a fixer or translator or aid worker in the area, so she was well-connected, and the other was a Palestinian Iraqi who was very well-connected to the resistance. I think that it was four or five weeks, but there would be a few days where maybe I would go to a Shia neighborhood and hang out with friends or something. And there were many, many slow days where nothing would happen and I'd just hang out with people.

Well, these weren't foreign fighters, and they weren't really Baathists. The commanders were a couple of clerics, and many of the people fighting were indeed from the former Iraqi military, but obviously these were the people who had military experience. The most important thing is I think they believed they were fighting to defend their city, to defend their religion, to defend their homes, and not for any other reason. They really felt like their homes and city were under attack, and given what the Americans did to their homes and city, they were partially correct. And I met, later on, a very important foreign fighter and go-between, between Saudi money and the Iraqi resistance, who was in Fallujah during the war and the days following the war trying to rally people to fight the occupation.

At the time right after the war, the Americans were in Fallujah the next couple weeks, and the Fallujans, the tribal leaders and clerics, just took over the city and ran the services and the administration peacefully and successfully. And they refused to fight the Americans, which frustrated the foreign fighters who had come in there hoping to start a fight. They wanted to give the Americans a chance and I think just wanted peace and something better. So American atrocities and rumors of American atrocities convinced the Fallujans to fight. It wasn't like Fallujah was something special—some special town that had something unique about it to let it be a powerful center for the insurgency. It was that first American massacre, the Iraqi response to it, the American responses to the Iraqi responses, which were just so brutal. Obviously there were foreign fighters, but a very small number until—and it wasn't that important until it just became an all-out war for survival. I mean, [in April 2004] we really destroyed that city of three hundred thousand people.

There were large neighborhoods that had just been destroyed, hospitals had been shot up, ambulances had been shot up, ambulance drivers had been killed—this was the first assault, April 2004—marines, and they just shot everything they could find.

That was the peak of Sunni-Shia unity against the Americans—May, June 2004. [The foreign fighters were] only in one neighborhood really, and they were clashing with the local fighters because there was just a conflict of—ideologically they were far more extreme, the foreigners, and they had a very different agenda. The dominant resistance movement wanted power over Fallujah and wanted the Americans out of there. So the last thing they wanted was more provocation. They wanted to preserve the status quo: once the Americans left, they'd maintain their power. And the foreign fighters were doing things to provoke the Americans and to extend the battle, and they were also much more of the Taliban in their position of Islam, whereas Fallujans tend to be Sufi—just a little more moderate.

HANNAH ALLAM | KNIGHT RIDDER (McCLATCHY)

I think of the beheading of Nicholas Berg [in May 2004]. And then after that it really seemed almost overnight. I guess it was the realization that reporters were not immune as targets. That we were considered foreigners, there was no distinction. That what we are doing here is noble and truth-telling, there was no distinction. A foreigner is a foreigner is a foreigner.

VIVIENNE WALT | FREELANCE WRITER

In the summer of 2004 I was working on a piece for *Time* about the rapid rise in honor killings in Iraq since the invasion. It ran in *Time* in July 2004, so I guess this might have been June that I was out reporting it. And I was in a hospital, in fact, and by that stage I had begun to go everywhere dressed in a long, black abaya, to try and disguise myself, and I would say I began to do that from, say, March of 2004. So I was in a full, black abaya in this hospital, the Al Kindi Hospital in East Baghdad, and I was interviewing women about how difficult their lives had become, and it was to put the issue of honor killings in perspective. And I was sitting out in some kind of corridor, interviewing women doctors, and of course somebody presumably overheard that I was speaking English. I came out. It was summer. It was very, very hot in Baghdad and my translator and I stepped outside the hospital gate and bought some fruit juice from a fruit-juice vendor on the sidewalk, and got back in the car and went out to lunch. By the way, all of these things would be extremely impossible to do now, I mean, we would never be buying fruit juice on the sidewalk, we'd never be going out to lunch in a restaurant in Baghdad.

But anyway, there we were, we went out to lunch, my driver, my translator, and I, and we got outside and the guards outside the restaurant that we were eating at came up to my driver and translator and said there was a car full of armed gunmen who were seen looking for this woman that you work for and want to know if she's an American. The guards at the restaurant actually knew me because we used to eat there quite regularly, and said "No, she's Lebanese," which was quite smart of them because Lebanese look somewhat different too. And from there we went to interview one of the local political leaders and when we left his office, the same car was sniffing around, looking for us, so we

In Baghdad, an Iraqi policeman guards the body of a murder victim. The man was apparently hung from a balcony by a rope tied around his foot and then dropped to his death. June 11, 2004. Stefan Zaklin/European Pressphoto Agency

headed back to the hotel and I didn't go out for a couple of days, and I believe, if I'm not mistaken, we switched cars—we got rid of the car that we were driving and got ourselves a new car. That was the time when I suddenly began to realize that my movements were being watched, and that more than that, if you stay around Baghdad long enough, you get to be a known quantity and you get to be watched. I think that's the moment at which it really struck me that this wasn't like other conflicts that I'd covered, and it wasn't a matter of being cautious about the wrong time and the wrong place, and that actually we were targets ourselves.

I happened to leave Baghdad some time after this piece about honor killings was published in *Time*, and I happened to hear from friends and contacts in Baghdad that the piece had actually made the rounds in Baghdad and had actually been spoken about in the mosques and I was advised that I should stay out of Baghdad for while. So yeah—the other thing that we tend to forget is that people are on the Internet a lot and we're kind of known quantities to people in Baghdad much more than we think we are.

ANDREW LEE BUTTERS |
FREELANCE WRITER
Mosul was in the throes of a growing insurgency, and this was at a time in the run-up to the election in the United States in 2004, in the late summer. George Bush was telling the American public that the war was going well and that most of the country was

safe, and Iyad Allawi, the prime minister of Iraq, was on the steps of the White House and was in the Rose Garden with George Bush telling the American public that there were only three dangerous provinces in Iraq and that the rest of the country was safe. You might have to check that. I think they were about three. Iyad Allawi was saying that almost the entire country was safe and that there were only a few problems. And I knew that Mosul, which is the third largest city in Iraq, was anything but safe. Doctors in the city's main hospitals were saying that they were getting three headless bodies delivered to the morgue everyday, and I was hearing about the systematic assassinations of professional and intellectual classes in Mosul, and generally threats against anyone who spoke out for freedom and democracy....

And I wrote this story, and it ended up not running in *Time* magazine because of another story from Samarra where the Americans mounted an operation to retake Samarra. My story ended up just going on the Web site. Now it turned out that I was absolutely right, and the falling of Mosul to the insurgency [was] really a huge story because when the Americans went to take Fallujah, the jihadis headed up north to Mosul, and half the police force joined up with them. Americans had to divert soldiers to Mosul.

LIZ SLY | *CHICAGO TRIBUNE*
We got hit by a rocket once [at the *Chicago*

Tribune house in Baghdad in May 2004], and it wasn't clear at the time whether the rocket was aimed at us or not, so it probably wasn't, but it was a good idea to be on the safe side. Also, all the windows and the front gate were blown off, so it wasn't safe to stay there in the short term. And the second time we moved because of the kidnappings, that was in September 2004, when they suddenly started snatching foreigners left and right and center, and we realized a news organization cannot provide sufficient security at one's house, you're better off moving to a hotel and leverage the bigger security the hotel can provide. And the third time we moved it was because our office was completely destroyed by a suicide bombing.

I was asleep, we had a couple of little hotel rooms, they were suite hotel rooms with little bedrooms attached to them. We had two of those rooms and I was asleep in the back bedroom that was least damaged in all the rooms of ours, so I was pretty lucky in that sense. I was blown out of bed and realized the floor next to the bed was the safest place, so I just stayed put because I knew there would be a second blast, which there was, and the second blast was enormous. The ceiling was crashing down and everything, but I was trapped in the corner and quite safe. My translator and his brother, the driver, the two who [had] just lost their sister, they were sleeping in the rooms directly over the bombing. And they were pretty shaken up. One of them went into a state of shock and basically couldn't

move for five days. The other was covered in cuts, lots of little cuts. The walls, the ceiling, everything came crashing down. It was quite a miraculous survival for them. And the ceilings came down, the water pipes burst, it was a big mess that we had to clean up.

DAN MURPHY |
THE CHRISTIAN SCIENCE MONITOR

Probably the way Fallujah was leveled [in November 2004] was not as well reported or understood as it could have been. But press had great access to that story. They were there. They were banging away with the marines, so they saw a lot. And there was an incredible amount of destruction in that city. And you have to remember you didn't have to be in Fallujah to cover the Iraqi side of the story. There were a lot of refugees that fled Fallujah and came to a refugee camp right up the road from where I'm staying. Of course, the people who ran that refugee camp took to kidnapping foreign reporters who wanted to talk about the situations those families found themselves in. So that story got a lot less coverage as time went on because they were shooting the messenger. But you know we did a couple of stories about them. We tried.

ELIZABETH PALMER | CBS NEWS

In the battle of Fallujah, it was one of the first times the Iraqi forces, the newly trained Iraqi forces, were deployed with the American soldiers. Two of these new Iraqi special forces soldiers were given to our unit, and the officers who were concentrating on the battle made absolutely no effort to integrate them, to give them the equipment they needed; they didn't even have body armor; they didn't have sleeping bags. There was no understanding that these guys, these Iraqis, would be their best allies in the field, that it was important to find out where they were from, whether they were Shia or Sunni, and what their unit was. I was able to write some of this for the Web page, but it never made it into mainstream television news because that needed to be the headline, the big story of the day. This is more peripheral stuff that's softer—very telling—but certainly not hard.

NIR ROSEN | FREELANCE WRITER

It was Shia-supported Fallujans in the first battle in April or May 2004, but [in] the second battle of Fallujah there was no Shia support, and Sunnis complained about that because it was apparent that Shias were just indifferent. And part of it was I think that they were just sick of the people who were associated with Fallujah and in general the Western province, the Anbar province, killing Shia civilians or killing the police or Shias or attacking the Iraqi Army—who were mostly Shias. So at some point they were just sick of Fallujah and didn't really mind that it was being destroyed. And Sunnis resented the Shia indifference in the second battle of Fallujah. And the areas where the Fallujans moved into in western Baghdad were already ones that tended to support the resistance and maybe more inclined to view Shias in a slightly negative way—they were Sunni majority areas, they were areas that were dominated by former Sunni military people. So the line between criminality and just wanting a cheap house, and hating Shias and wanting them out of your neighborhood—those intersected, and a lot of the sectarian clan things started in those days when the Sunni refugees came looking for homes and they were already pissed off at Shias anyway.

In particular, Amiriyah, which is the area where, you might remember, in 1991 [during the First Gulf War] an Iraqi bomb shelter was hit, a lot of civilians were killed. So that's right in the center of Amiriyah. It's an area that's predisposed to be anti-American already because of the nature of the population, and it's in western Baghdad, where the suburbs are most, and a lot of people have relatives in the Anbar province and Fallujah or themselves come from there one or two generations before. So they invited their relatives from Fallujah to come stay there. And you're talking thousands of families, because Fallujah virtually was empty—it went from like three hundred thousand to like thirty thousand or less.

I really believe that fall 2004, was the beginning of—we'll leave the Kurdish areas out for now—that was the beginning of the civil war. That's when ethnic cleaning really got started. The first stories you heard of Shias being pushed from their homes, of getting letters, of their homes being bombed. It all started, I think, in the western parts of Baghdad—Amiriyah, Abu Ghraib, places like that—with the Sunni refugees.

GHAITH ABDUL-AHAD | *THE GUARDIAN,* GETTY IMAGES

I remember that day in Fallujah [embedded with insurgents, in November 2004]. It's raining. The night before the town was bombed—it was a really rough night—we didn't sleep. And in the morning I was sitting in this yard outside the house we were staying in, and there was this Yemeni guy, and he was a normal guy, he is a guy that you would meet everywhere. And this guy was cleaning his weapons. I was sitting next to him, taking a couple shots of him cleaning his weapons, taking pictures, and it was raining.

And then the guy started talking, and he was telling his story, how he grew up and why he came to Iraq. And this guy was part of one of the Arab jihadis coming from all over the world, coming to Iraq, coming to fight in Fallujah. I felt so weird. It wasn't my first experience with insurgents but it was as if someone just opened a door, and suddenly I was on the other side. And I was seeing what was happening. The guy was telling me his story, he kept talking and I was taking notes and writing. And I was so overwhelmed by what I was hearing, not because it's an amazing story—it's just the story of this Yemeni man and how he came to Syria and was smuggled across Iraq, it's the same story that we all knew, how jihadis were

coming—but it was on a personal level, it was him talking about his family back in Yemen, him saying goodbye to his little daughter without telling her that he was going to Iraq to die, the personal level of the story. And that was just like really weird and amazing to understand the personal background of those people and why they were there fighting.

Of course, there were these moments when they went to pray and they asked me to go and pray, and I said, "No, no thank you, I don't pray," and they were trying to tell me why I should pray. And then this other guy comes, and he listens to this whole conversation and of people preaching to me and trying to convince me to pray. And then he's asking, "What's wrong with him?" and they're saying, "He's not praying." "Why?" "Because he's not a Muslim." And then he's just kind of naturally saying, "Why don't we kill him?" the same way you would say, "Oh, why don't you have a cup of tea? Why don't you kill that fly on your shoulder?" He is just asking, "Why don't we kill him?" and they are saying, "No, no, no, we are in a kind of truce with him. We can't kill him because we gave him the truce, we gave him permission to stay with us." And it's just these little moments where you leave Fallujah, and like two years after Fallujah you are thinking, "What was I thinking?" And I was like "Fucking hell, what did I do to myself?" I was like sitting with those guys, and "Why don't we kill him?"

NIR ROSEN | FREELANCE WRITER

In my travels through the Muslim world, and
Pakistan and Somalia, even, I would hear
about this myth of Fallujah—they wiped
out the city. And to Sunnis that was very
important to hear, the evidence that there
was a war against Sunnis, to annihilate them.
And throughout the Muslim world, Fallujah
had so much resonance that the word and
the meaning and the symbolism of it now—
it's like a Muslim Masada, I think.

VII

THE EMBEDS

DAN MURPHY |
THE CHRISTIAN SCIENCE MONITOR
Embedding is a fancy word for letting
journalists go see what the military units do,
although that was much more wide open in
the Vietnam War, although that was much
more of an anomaly of American history.
It was much more locked down in the First
Gulf War, clearly. And now there is a bit of
bureaucracy you have to go through and
sometimes [the military] wants to steer you
in some direction or another direction, but
in general, in my personal experience—I
guess I've probably done, maybe five
embeds—I've always learned new things and
I've always gotten great access to intelligence
guys who'll give you off-the-record briefings
in the area and talk about what their points
of concern are as well as what they think is
going well. I've always found it fascinating.
I consider it an incredible privilege in
many ways to go out and see what these
guys do. Unless you are a soldier yourself,
very few people ever get to see infantrymen
in combat. I'm into that and feel very
privileged to do it. The only limitation is
you are going where they want to go, on
their schedules. You are not going to get all
the access you want or be able to do all you
want. And you are not going to get to talk to
Iraqis when you do this.

COLONEL WILLIAM DARLEY |
MILITARY REVIEW
Well, embedding is a tremendous thing
for public affairs officers. Every embed is

a straw. You're seeing the war through a straw. So it's a good thing for the military. The more straws you can get out there, the more coverage, I think, the better. The military's not going to succeed unless it has political—and certainly in connection with that—public support. If you don't have political support, if you don't have public support—the translation of political support—the military can't succeed. And in the military, there's no way the military can tell its own story. Every once in a while they think they can, like this Pentagon channel that we have. I don't watch it and I get it, because it's a constant, unremitting flow of propaganda and it's not interesting, and people don't have recourse to it. For all the badmouthing that the American public does to the media, they depend on them. It's the lifeblood.

PATRICK COCKBURN | *THE INDEPENDENT* (LONDON)

I think it's a great mistake to go with American units and report on any Iraqi city because I think it's in the nature of things that you're not actually meeting local people, and if you are, you aren't meeting them in circumstances in which they can actually speak.

TOM LASSETER | KNIGHT RIDDER (McCLATCHY)

To me, not embedding is like not going to a mosque. I can't imagine going to Iraq without spending the time I've spent in

mosques there. And I can't imagine having gone to Iraq without spending the time that I've spent embedding.

MITCH PROTHERO | UNITED PRESS INTERNATIONAL

I'm a staunch defender of these [embedding] programs. I don't think it's a substitute for anything. It is what it is. It's reporting on what it's like to be with that frontline unit. I think that's what it should be seen as and that's invaluable. Go back to 1991 and look at the news coverage of [the Persian Gulf War] when [the Americans] went in. Essentially everybody was locked up in Saudi [Arabia] getting these obscure press briefings and the American people had virtually no idea what was going on if it wasn't for a handful of crazy guys with the SUVs driving around the desert. I mean I think it's invaluable and I think it's something that the media owes the soldiers to a certain extent and I think it's helped the relationship between the media and the soldiers, and the media and the military because you know we have a better understanding of what it's like to be a U.S. soldier and you need to understand your subject.

Let's say a civilian Iraqi car gets shot up at a checkpoint. Obviously this is a huge tragedy, but is it a crime? Well, if you've never been embedded you're not going to understand the procedure, you're not going to understand the mentality, and you're not going to understand that gut fear that you have when you're sitting in Humvees and the car doesn't stop, for whatever reason, whether it's because they're a suicide bomber or because it's a confused, panicked Iraqi guy. If you want to cover the stuff, you have to know what that feels like before you do anybody justice, whether you're trying to do justice to the Iraqis or to the Americans.

NIR ROSEN | FREELANCE WRITER

The two weeks [in October 2003] that I was [embedded with the U.S. Army] I saw many things that broke my heart and made me angry, and there have been journalists who have been embedded for many, many months during the occupation throughout areas where there are a lot of operations, so they must have seen so many more things than I did. Each time [the soldiers] go on a raid they break down the walls in front of the house; they break down the door, they drag the men out—it's a very violent, horrifying thing. And usually these are large families. So in the middle of the night you have these huge Martian-looking soldiers breaking into the house when you're asleep, dragging your father out, stowing all the women to one side, not really speaking your language, pointing guns at you, stomping all over your house in their boots, and they've just learned that it's not even the right house. In my experience, they arrested hundreds more men than they were looking for. They basically arrested all the men. At some point they arrested all the men in the town, it seemed, that were fighting age.

VIVIENNE WALT | FREELANCE WRITER

I was on patrol one night [in March 2004] with a platoon [from the First Armored Cavalry Division], and we were in the town of Abu Ghraib, which is next to the prison of Abu Ghraib. And the platoon, towards dawn—they'd spent all night kind of dragging people out of bed, looking for weapons, and it was unclear what they were looking for. It was just kind of an all-night raid on this town, and the platoon leader turned out to be kind of antiwar in general. All night [he] was saying to me, "I don't know why the fuck we're here." You know, that was his big line. "What the hell are we here for? I don't know why the fuck we're here. They actually thought Saddam had weapons of mass destruction here—give me a break, what a joke." You know, I was writing in my notebook all the time, and he didn't care—and it was, I thought, a very important piece of the story, that not all U.S. soldiers are gung-ho about the war. And it got toward dawn and they decided to do one last raid on one last house, and they get to this big metal gate. The gate is padlocked and there's this little dog yapping away, and it's like four in the morning, the whole town is asleep, and the sergeant of the platoon goes nuts—he's exhausted and crabby and starts screaming, "Shut the fucking dog up!" you know, and then finally, he pushed at the gates, he pushed the chain open a few inches and put his rifle through and fired a shot and mortally wounded this dog.

So then they shoot open the lock and the

dog's lying there bleeding and the platoon leader, who was the one who was somewhat antiwar, and who also turned out to be a big dog-lover, went completely nuts. You know the dog was like in terrible, terrible pain, and so he leaned over and basically delivered a mercy shot to this dog, by which time the owner of the house has come out and is sort of standing there in shock, and there were twenty armed American soldiers standing in his front yard and his dog was dead. So the whole thing was just a total mess, and then the platoon leader started shouting, "Why the hell did you shoot the dog, are you nuts?" and the other guy said, "It's none of your business." They actually took their helmets off and they laid into each other, physically. And then the other soldiers separated them.

We got back to the base at breakfast time, and I wrote an account of what had happened that night—the whole night was sort of interesting—which then wound up being a front-page lead story in *The Boston Globe*, as a result of which, this guy, who was the platoon leader, was court-martialed [it was eventually dropped after he resigned his commission]. So, the whole thing turned out to be a big incident from what had really been somewhat of a minor, passing incident in the greater scheme of things. Some of my colleagues sort of said, actually did say to me, "Oh, you might have kind of damaged our relations with this platoon." And in fact I then subsequently went back to see the platoon, just to make sure I hadn't damaged

anybody's relationship. And it didn't seem like I had.

JANE ARRAF | CNN

A story of Samarra again, with the military, embedded, that they had facilitated, where we went to the hospital and, lo and behold, there are women and children who are dead. We are able to do a story, at this morgue at this hospital, with pictures showing, that yes, there were civilian casualties. Not only did the military allow us to do that, they also took us to the cemetery, where they dropped us off some distance and again handed us over to Iraqi soldiers and we watched them bury their dead. Some of the soldiers complained, but there was no fallout because I'd explained to the commanders what I was doing. I had been upfront, I wasn't pretending I'd seen anything else. The best of them, the thing they demand from you is that you are fair and you are accurate.

One story I was able to do while embedded—again facilitated by the military—was this story on this extraordinary man whose entire family was killed by U.S. soldiers. They fired on him. It's a long way of saying, being embedded is not to have blinders on.

MARTIN SMITH | FRONTLINE

I had an interesting embed up outside of Kirkuk, where our cameraman went out into a small town where [American forces] were rooting out some insurgents, and he was filming them as they were destroying the house of an old couple. Inside the house they had found some explosives, some other materials, guns and whatnot, and the old couple would not tell them where the son was. And so they said, "Okay, you're not going to tell us where your son is, then we'll destroy your house." Well, that started to make them think hard; as the front wall came down, they relented. Now, the [soldier who] was in charge of that operation at first said, "You can't film this," and then the commander stepped in and said, "No, this is what we do, they have a right to film this." That was a very instructive little episode; not all commanders would allow it. Another incident, very early on: we were running around Baghdad early on and we came upon this scene where soldiers were confronting some guys who were looting some wood, and they clearly didn't have training for this situation, and they decided that the way to punish these people is to yell at them in English, so they didn't understand, and then take their car and crush it with their tank.

And it became a kind of, in a small way, iconic, because it was brought up to [Deputy Secretary of Defense Paul] Wolfowitz later— who claimed it was being investigated, I never saw any results from that—but that was a scene where the soldiers thought what they were doing was a wonderful thing...I don't think if any political figure from CPA or a ranking commander above a colonel level had seen what we were filming, they would have certainly been very uncomfortable with it and either asked us to stop filming or

instructed the soldiers. But there was enough chaos and enough people not knowing what their role was, that it was not always easy for them to control what you filmed and what you didn't.

GHAITH ABDUL-AHAD | *THE GUARDIAN,* GETTY IMAGES

I had spent two weeks on an embed, and then I went out in the raid, and one of the soldiers in the raid realized that I speak Arabic, because I was trying to translate what an old woman was trying to tell him. And I had a nice, good relationship with those guys because I was with them for, I don't know, a week with that specific unit, and I built up a relationship with the guys. We were joking, chatting, but the moment they realized that I spoke the language, this whole trust disappeared and there was a huge wall put up between us. And the next day I found myself in another base in the middle of the desert, and I had to ask to end my embed. And I believe they don't trust someone who can talk to the others. In another embed I was sitting in a room waiting—I was doing an embed with the Iraqi Army, and to do an embed with the Iraqi Army you have to go through the U.S, and I was sitting in the American base waiting to be picked up by the Iraqi unit. And there was this captain sitting in front of his computer and he said "What's your name?" and I gave him my name, and after two minutes, he said, "Huh, so you've done a fair amount of reporting on the other side." He did a Google search. And I

Five-year-old Samar Hassan screams after her
parents were killed by U.S. soldiers in Tal Afar.
Soldiers with the Twenty-fifth Infantry Division
fired on the Hassan family car as it unwittingly
approached them during a dusk patrol. Her brother
was paralyzed from the waist down and was later
treated in the U.S. January 18, 2005.
Chris Hondros/Getty Images

think Google is a very bad—it's immediately uncensored, immediately people know your background. So I realized from that day that when I'm embedded with the U.S Army, since I speak Arabic, they don't trust you.

COLONEL WILLIAM DARLEY |
MILITARY REVIEW

I only know of one reporter, one embed, that was briefly expelled. It was someone from *The Wall Street Journal.* It was a disagreement about what was on or off the record. That's the only incident I know. I know lots of reporters that have written pretty damning reports from what they objectively believe they found. That other guy from *The Wall Street Journal*, Greg Jaffe, he wrote a scathing article with regard to Iraqi training and the success of Iraqi soldiers with the Eighty-second Airborne Division. It was really a downer. Nobody took any retribution against him. He's still welcome back. He's still invited back because he's known to be a straight shooter. On balance, we have a pretty mature group of colonels and generals who recognize that if there's a turd in the bowl, and somebody reports the turd, well, that's the price of doing business with an embed.

CHRIS HONDROS | GETTY IMAGES

By and large, the embed program—three and a half years into it—is still remarkably important, and while it has had problems here and there—there have been cases of soldiers confiscating someone's sat [satellite] phone, taking media cards to prevent pictures from going out—so much has come out, so much of our understanding of Iraq has come from embeds. I mean, my God, the battle of Fallujah—that was 100 percent covered by sixty, seventy journalists embedded with the U.S. military. We think we don't know anything about Iraq now. Man, if we didn't have embeds, we wouldn't know anything about Iraq! And the notion that you sort of start identifying with troops and stuff like that when you're relying on them for your security, well that's true to some extent, but again, in ways that are true for any journalist covering anything.

Luckily for journalists, the military is not nearly as organized or centralized as people would like to think. In November 2003, there was a French photographer, Jerome Sessini, who was doing a sort of embed with insurgents. And he would claim that he never knew where he was going to go, and one day [the insurgents] said, "Okay, come with us, we're gonna go someplace," and he goes with them and they pull out to a field by the airport and whip out a big missile, a missile-launching tube, and they said, "Yeah, we're going to shoot down an airplane." And he's sitting there thinking, he says, "Oh my God, what can I do?" And he was worried that they would just kill him. So he had no choice. So he photographs them setting up and then you see the guy—there's a picture of the missile coming out of the tube, and then a picture of the plane getting hit in the sky—it was a cargo plane, a DHL cargo plane taking off from Baghdad airport—and the flames bursting out of the wings. On a side note, three very talented pilots actually managed to land that plane with only one engine—on fire—and they were okay.

And then he had them celebrating in the fields and all that. And then he went back, and was in a bit of a daze, and he sent the pictures to his agency, who distributed them and they ran all over magazines. *Newsweek International* ran them; European and Asian *Newsweek* ran them as a big double spread. The military saw them—the U.S. military— and was furious that a western journalist was with insurgents who are shooting down coalition aircrafts. Who is this guy? The military was literally looking to arrest him and bring him in to question him. So this guy basically got in a car and took off, and went on the road to Jordan and escaped from Baghdad.

Okay, that was October 2003, around there. By around fall 2004, I come back, and there was Jerome hanging out in our office. "What you been up to?" "Oh, I was doing an embed on Haifa Street," which is in downtown—a U.S. military-patrolled street in downtown Baghdad that saw a lot of action. And he was embedded in Haifa Street—when you were embedded in Haifa Street, you didn't have to actually stay with them on their base. You could just drive up there, go embed, and then come back and stay in the hotel at night. And he was doing that with one of our photographers, Joe Raedle, and anyway he was doing embeds! This guy, who

a year before had the entire U.S. military looking for him, was doing embeds in Baghdad!

ANTHONY SHADID |
THE WASHINGTON POST
I've heard stories about articles being graded according to certain colors whether they're favorable or not, favorable or neutral. I think there's a certain abuse going on within the embedding system at this point. I think this is something we need to be writing about.

And more and more, we're becoming combatants. As reporters, we're losing this noncombatant status. And it was much different—I remember back in Afghanistan in 1997, there was no question I was off limits. Even hanging out with the Taliban fighters outside Kabul, you were off limits. Just in ten years that I've been doing this, I think it's dramatic how much more we're considered combatants. And it's not just insurgents in Iraq, but I think also the U.S. military. I think we're only looking at it in its embryonic form, but if you look ten, fifteen years down the road, there might be a sense that reporters are either embedded and therefore legitimate or unembedded and therefore illegitimate.

DEXTER FILKINS | *THE NEW YORK TIMES*
But by and large, by dint of what you've done, I mean as a consequence of what you've signed up for, you're essentially part of the military. Certainly in the eyes of Iraqis

you are—you're not wearing a uniform but you're with them, you're surrounded by guys with guns, so you're basically talking to soldiers. Yeah, you can break away; you can—if you're embedded…most of the time you're not fighting, right? Most of the time it's reasonably calm and you're sitting around at a base, so you're with a civil affairs officer who says, "Look, I've got this reconstruction project that I'm doing in this village and why don't you come with me?" and you go and he sits down and he talks to the Iraqis about the water project that they're building. Now, you can talk to the Iraqis then; now you're probably not going to—you can't really assume—the guy probably, the Iraqi guy, if he's smart he's going to say, "We love the Americans and they're great and they'll give us a lot of money." You can't assume that that's his honest opinion, but having said that, that is a huge limitation of embedding. You have to do it if you're going to go to—it's just a fact of life now, that for any one of us to go to Iraq, or I mean to go anywhere in the Sunni Triangle, we've got to embed. But that does not mean that you can't either talk to Iraqis or talk to them later or send Iraqis in to the very place where you are to talk to them, or as I've done before with Unit X in Ramadi, actually have them actually bring Iraqis from Ramadi to our house in Baghdad so that I can talk to them myself. It's unbelievably cumbersome and ridiculous and expensive and time-consuming, but we can do it, we can

PATRICK GRAHAM | FREELANCE WRITER
In Sadr City during that uprising in [April] 2004, one thing you did learn [from embedding] was how isolated the U.S. troops were from their environment, which was something. You always got the impression from the outside, but being in the Bradleys, driving around and shooting people at night, you really could see how far… At the same time, and it's such a dilemma, I really admired the battlefield command of the U.S. Army: the captains, the lieutenants were incredibly impressive and smart. But you could see yourself being really sympathetic to these people, and…you learn something. The thing I learned most from embedding was that the distance between the U.S. Army and the locals was unbridgeable.

GHAITH ABDUL-AHAD | *THE GUARDIAN*, GETTY IMAGES
Leftists, Maoists, nationalist—insurgents are always perceived as the people who really need the media to cover their insurgency and to boost their case. But insurgents, at this moment, and we're talking about the Islamic fundamentalist insurgents who are now in Iraq, they don't like journalism. It is always seen as tainted, a product of the West, as a propaganda to the West. So that's the first thing, they don't like journalism, they don't trust journalists. And they don't need us, they don't need journalism, they have the Internet. They film their own operations, it's a strategy I think started by Hezbollah in the '80s, where they were kind of going

out and filming their own operations. Why would they need a journalist to go out with them, embed with them quote unquote, and film their operations, jeopardize their security, someone who they don't trust? It's this absolutist Islamic ideology of…they don't like us. And they are doing the job themselves. So on the insurgent side this is why they don't like us.

And on the American side I think this concept of invading has tainted this whole profession of journalism for an American soldier. And I've had this conversation with so many American soldiers, and they ask me "Do you walk on your own in the street? You don't carry weapons? And you live in the Red Zone?" They can't perceive that journalists are supposed to cover the two sides. The other side is kind of called terrorist, they are criminals, how can you as a journalist cover the other side, it should be with us. Because they see journalists embedding with them, and they can't perceive journalists as being independent, covering the two sides and crossing the line.

LARRY KAPLOW | COX NEWSPAPERS

A lot of times, when you go to an American installation, and they know that you're just walking out their gates into your private car to drive away, they'll say they wish they could do that. And they really would like to know the kinds of things we see out there.

PAUL HOLMES | REUTERS

I do think there is an institutional resistance at a senior level in the serving military on this conflict to engage with the media, and I don't think it comes from a disdain from the media. I think it comes from the situation in Iraq, I think it comes to some degree from the system of embedding, which I think has—we welcome embedding, we always did and we always welcome embedding. We've never regarded embedding as the only way to gather news in Iraq.

I think there are two possible responses. One is the ordinary soldiers, who as a result of embedding might believe, "The journalists who are embedded with us are good journalists and the journalists who are not embedded with us might not be good journalists." And I think there's—at senior levels of the military—I don't think there's a clear understanding of what the role of a journalist is, necessarily, and therefore there's a view, "If you embed, you'll be safe, we'll give you access," which is true, you do get an awful lot of access within the military. You're obviously not able to cover the insurgents and you're not able to cover ordinary Iraqis. And there's not sufficient appreciation at senior levels that journalists need to operate independently; we and our journalists go to Iraq on our own responsibility, and we've always made clear to the military that we are not asking the military to be responsible for the safety of our staff. That's unrealistic and it's unreasonable of us. What we are asking for is the military to engage with us to minimize the risks and to treat journalists like noncombatant civilians. And that has proven very, very difficult to achieve.

MITCH PROTHERO |
UNITED PRESS INTERNATIONAL

I did an interview on a Fox News program under which they had written underneath my picture and my name, Mitch Prothero, Baghdad Bureau Chief from United Press, in giant letters, "embedded with the terrorists." Well, I reported on the Mahdi Army, and I was on the Fox News explaining who these guys were, what they were angry about, why they were suddenly fighting the Americans, when the Americans had been lead to believe the Shia were all very supportive of their presence in Iraq, and here were hundreds, if not thousands of young men going out into the streets demonstrating, and in many cases fighting. Yeah, I was "embedded with the terrorists." Which is a misnomer on both counts. And because of that I got a bunch of nice e-mails from people. I've been threatened with death from the right, I've been called a Bush apologists and hack by the left.

PATRICK COCKBURN | *THE INDEPENDENT*
(LONDON)

In November 2004 the U.S. Marines surrounded and captured Fallujah. Many foreign journalists were embedded with the marines and reported on this and it was well reported; there were excellent reports from many people. But it was also presented as a victory, which is reasonable enough,

but then also presented as a victory which showed that insurgents were on the run. Now, it so happens I know Mosul quite well. The population of Fallujah is 350,000 max; Mosul is about 1.7 million, so it's a much bigger city. Now, the attack on Fallujah was on 7 November 2004. Four days later, on 11 November, the insurgents attacked Mosul and captured it. They captured thirty police stations: the entire police force either defected or went home. One brigade of the Iraqi Army also evaporated. This was a major defeat, which happened at the same time. Now nobody was embedded with the U.S. forces and nobody really reported it. There were a few scattered reports but it made no impact abroad, but this is extremely significant because it showed that whatever had happened in Fallujah, the insurgents were still powerful and capable of taking a large city.

ANNE BARNARD | *THE BOSTON GLOBE*

Embedding is a tool and so by itself it's neutral—it depends how you use it, and in what context you use it. So I don't think you can say embedding has been good or bad. I think for me embedding has been a really extremely useful tool for several reasons. First of all, embedding is most effective as a way of understanding what's going on in Iraq if you have a context to put it in, if you yourself have traveled around Iraq, if you have locals who can help you report outside of the embed bubble, in the same place, if you have experience going back where

Iraqi soldiers and U.S. military
advisers patrol the Haifa Street
neighborhood in Baghdad.
March 17, 2005. Yuri Kozyrev

you understand what that place has been through from a different perspective from the embeds.

From the very beginning, in April 2003, I had regularly gone out to Fallujah and met people there. I went into Fallujah again, right after the battle [in November 2004] with a civil-affairs team that was trying to put the city back together. And it was sort of a scary reenactment of the original Iraq invasion, a microcosm of the Iraq invasion. Here were civil-affairs teams that were going in, and they were supposed to rebuild the whole city, but they hadn't been given any plans, any blueprints, any understanding of which ministries were responsible for what. And these were marines who were suddenly supposed to make the banking system work and the plumbing system work and the water system. It already looked like a recipe for disaster, so I went back later and I tried to write in a textured way about what they'd achieved and what they were not achieving, but that was only two or three months after the battle was over, and that was the last time I personally was there.

So when I watched the coverage—and this goes back to the limitations of embeds— you can see that people are going on embeds to Fallujah, for say a week, and people are writing, "Fallujah is suddenly much better now than a couple months ago," and then another article will say, "Fallujah, it's a real disappointment," and it almost depends on what that person's benchmark is. You can almost tell from the story whether the person—or at least it raises the question when you read the story: Was this person in Fallujah before Fallujah became an insurgent stronghold? Was this person in Fallujah before the first aborted invasion attempt? Was this person in Fallujah during the battle? Was this person in Fallujah immediately after the battle? Are they with soldiers who just arrived? Or with soldiers who just left? Or are they with soldiers who know that they are near the end of their tour, soldiers who came in with these high hopes for how much they were going to achieve and it hasn't been nearly achieved, and now they're leaving.

That's a limitation of embedding— that you're seeing a snapshot of a place. A snapshot of the military and how it operates. You know, I find it very instructive if you spend time with a unit when they first arrive to their area of operations—you should also go back and spend time with them at the end, and see whether they're still saying "our AO [area of operations] is one of the most successful ones in Iraq."

I don't mean to sound flippant, but these guys often come in saying that they've heard a lot about the problems but in this area the people really want to work with us, they really want to make a fresh start. And you don't want to be mean, but you say, "Well, you guys, I've been here and I've been with a lot of units and they all talk like you when they first arrive."

PETER MAASS |
THE NEW YORK TIMES MAGAZINE

These guys all check with each other when they're dealing with journalists. When I was trying to get American permission to embed in Samarra [in 2005], I was sending e-mails to headquarters in Tikrit, to officers there, officers in Baghdad, people in Washington, and then they were forwarding my e-mails back and forth. And then they would reply to me, and sometimes they would forget that there was a whole stream of messages between them, about me. And in one of these messages where they had been communicating with each other and had mistakenly included that in a reply to me, they had said, one of them said, "Well, I checked with," and he mentioned the name of a retired special forces guy here in America who I had talked with, and he said, "Oh, I checked with Khalev, and Khalev says he's okay, and I think we can probably support this." And so they're checking, okay?

But if you spend enough time, if you kind of reach a critical mass of knowledge about the military and people in the military, there is a level of great coordination. There's an elite in the military, among the military there are ones who are clearly sharp, who know what's going on, and can tell you what to do and who to go to and all of that. And those people are kind of permanent. And there are people who I can call in the army or the marines who will tell me, "Okay, you want to do this story, this is who you got to go to." And I'll send them an e-mail or something like that. So, yeah, the turnover is not good but you can always find out who's where and where to go to get people, even though you don't know the commanders who you want to have access to.

ANNE GARRELS | **NPR**

I was assigned to a battalion of marines and to a platoon that went in on foot, and it was, without doubt, the scariest thing I've ever done; the night before I wasn't sure I was going to be able to do it. It meant carrying fifty pounds on my back, and the marines clearly didn't want me, an old woman, and they didn't know what public radio was, for starters. If they were gonna have a correspondent, they wanted a guy from Fox. They did not want a fifty-four-year-old woman from NPR, about which they knew nothing. And all of us were scared the night before; this was really—we were much more exposed than I think we had ever dreamed.

And I still have nightmares, truth be told; posttraumatic, whatever you wanna call it. It doesn't come in direct ways, it comes in weird ways. After I got home, some kids were celebrating down at the lake just a few hundred yards from here, and they set off fireworks and I found myself curled up, just sobbing. I went skiing—and I'd been to this place in Utah a million times, and there are avalanche dangers and they blow the mountain to precipitate avalanches, and I've seen this for twenty years. Well, they did it this year and the next thing I know I'm in the arms of my stepdaughter sobbing my guts out. I don't have, I don't regularly have nightmares—it just comes in odd ways, subtle ways. Anger—all of us—I know I've had anger issues; they're hard to describe.

We were hit by RPGs [rocket-propelled grenades] walking through the streets, and kids were killed or injured on either side of me, you didn't have time at the time to reflect on it. It's only sort of later that you just go, "Jesus Christ," and I know from talking to the others, there were a handful of us who were in this sort of similar situation, basically on the ground with foot patrols, and I—just speaking for myself—will never do it again.

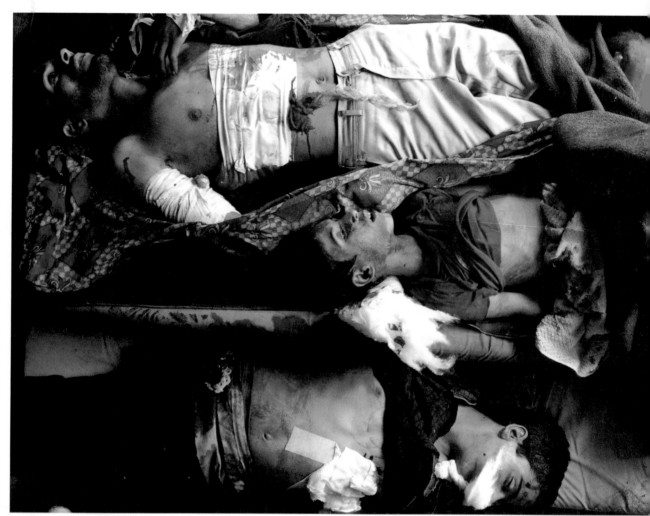

Iraqi corpses lie in a hospital morgue in Sadr
City after the Mahdi army, a militia loyal to the
Shiite cleric Moqtada al-Sadr, clashed with U.S.
forces when the militia attempted to take control
of government buildings and police stations in
the Baghdad neighborhood. April 5, 2004.
Stefan Zaklin/European Pressphoto Agency

VIII

REPORTING IN IRAQ

NIR ROSEN | FREELANCE WRITER
I met a young Iraqi guy [in April 2003], college student, secular Shia guy, very street-smart, from a poor family, who became a very close friend of mine and sort of trained me how to be Iraqi—taught me the Iraqi dialect, taught me things I needed to know to fit in in the mosques, fit in on the Iraqi streets. I sort of joined a local gym, mostly Shia neighborhood kids who worked out under horrible conditions. They were lifting bricks. But it was a great opportunity to mix with young men and hang out with them, go to restaurants with them, and because I was their age and I was into exercising, I got to get into the world of young Iraqi men. I never really made contact with young Iraqi women—I think that was mostly impossible. I think most did [know that I am an American], but I stressed the Iranian side of my ethnicity.

DEXTER FILKINS | *THE NEW YORK TIMES*
People will say, "If you print my name I'll be killed," and you know you have to believe that 'cause it happens all the time. It doesn't happen as much as you would think. It's remarkable how even now you can find people who will speak their minds. It's a lot harder. Iraqis are not as eager to talk to you as they used to be, but that usually is from an immediate fear they'll be seen with a westerner, rather than what somebody's going to read in the paper. People do not like to have their picture taken. I was just at an American military base in California where they set up these mock-Iraqi villages to train soldiers in guerilla warfare, and

they have Iraqi Americans working in these villages, these fake villages in California, and the Iraqis didn't want to talk because they were afraid that their families would be killed back in Iraq. Man, that was in California, so yeah, that happens all the time.

ALI FADHIL | TRANSLATOR, REPORTER
My background is I'm a physician. I graduated from medical school in 2001. I practiced medicine in Iraq and also in Yemen, and I returned to Iraq—I worked as a doctor in June 2003 until January 2004. By the end of the year I had a dual job to work as translator-fixer for the western journalists and as a doctor back in the hospital. My friend, Rory McCarthy, he is a Baghdad reporter for *The Guardian*; he's a very nice guy, but at the same time, he was a tyrant with me, and in fact he is the one who taught me how to be disciplined when I do a story or I do an interview. There is no way that I can miss questions, there is no way that you can just misrepresent something—you just hear something and you interpret in the way that you think it's right—no, you have to go and ask him again and again and again. And so he helped me a lot in figuring out these things.

PETER MAASS |
THE NEW YORK TIMES MAGAZINE
So, we drive down [to Najaf, in spring 2003], and our first stop is to see my interpreter's cousin in Najaf, and you know the way it is in Iraq. A family member will do everything he

can for you, even though this cousin—Tiar, my interpreter, hadn't seen him for two or three years. So we go there and the cousin is a small businessman there, and a really nice guy as it turns out. We sit down and have a tea and all that, and he says, "What can I do for you?" And Tiar says, "Is there anybody here who speaks English who can stay with Peter and work with Peter?" And so the cousin says, "Well, there aren't a lot of people who speak English here." The cousin doesn't speak English. He says, "But let me make some calls and ask." I forget the precise sequence, but within an hour we're at this hotel in Najaf, and this tiny little guy walks in, who's like an accounting professor at the local community college or whatever, who speaks English, not really, really well but speaks it. And he seems like a really, a nice guy, not the most confident guy, but a nice guy, and I figure—I'm with Ozier Muhammad, who's a staff photographer for the *Times*—and we say, "Okay, this could work."

So we send our interpreter home, and we have this local interpreter. And we're the first Americans he's ever met. Really. And you know, he's from Najaf, and he knows everybody as it turns out. And he was kind of a Sadrist. Sadr's office is right next to the Imam Ali shrine. So we go there, and there are guards out front, Sadr's own guards. The accountant knows the guards. We go inside the office, it's a tiny little building, it's like the Iraqi equivalent of a brownstone let's say, but not a brownstone. And my accountant knows some of the lower-level students who are there and others, and just talks with them. I talk with them. And all that kind of stuff, do the usual chit-chat. But my accountant is vouching for me, and so, long story short, a BBC crew arrives, and Sadr agrees to see us.

And so we go upstairs in his office and sit waiting in the office, and then Sadr walks in. We're talking with Sadr for forty-five minutes or an hour, and then at the end of the interview, because I didn't want to just have that, I said, "I want to stay and write about how you do what you do, and your interactions with the people because the people are very important to you and they look up to you." And Sadr said, "Okay, sure, alright." So then, for the rest of that day, for the next day, I just stayed in his headquarters, and he just sits on this cushion in a room, and people just kind of go up to him asking him for favors. "Can you lend me some money?" "The generator's not working in my store." All that kind of stuff.

I don't know what these people are saying to Sadr, but my digital tape recorder with a really good microphone is recording it all. What happens is, Sadr's sitting on the ground with his knees crossed, my tape recorder's right next to his knee. People come, sit right in front of him, and they almost prostrate themselves in front of him trying to kiss his hand—he doesn't let them do that—and then they have a whispered conversation. Sadr leans forward a little bit and the person's leaning right into him, and there's Sadr's knee and there's my tape recorder. Even if I spoke and understood Arabic, I would have to be leaning right over listening to what these guys are saying, which I couldn't do, even though I was sitting right next to Sadr; it would just have been a little bit obnoxious. So, I don't know what they're really saying, but at the end of the day we go back to my hotel room and listen to it on my tape recorder. And it's nothing, you know, they're not talking about matters of great national security, but it's like these people are asking him, "Can you give me some money?" or "This isn't working," or "How should we run this school?" and all that kind of stuff, and it was very colorful, and very useful.

You know, when I was in Afghanistan I was doing a profile on a warlord there, and I had lunch with him and his commanders. And I was sitting next to him, and I had a tape recorder, not digital but the regular tape recorders, and he was telling stories to his commanders. I didn't know what was going on because my interpreter actually wasn't there at that moment, and there was another guy who spoke a little bit of English but wasn't really interpreting. But my tape recorder was there.

DEBORAH AMOS | NPR

I always count what happened in Iraq by how I would dress. In the early days, in 2003, I dressed like I would in New York. Perhaps a little bit more modestly—long sleeves and long pants. But as time went on we had to now dress as Iraqi women, and the most conservative costumes Iraqi women would wear. Black abayahs, black head scarves. Still, the people who wanted to talk to you were not intimidated by microphones, not at all. If people were willing to talk to you they were willing to do it on the record. The problem was, could you get to them? And by 2004, early 2005, there were whole parts of Baghdad that were off limit to us, and our window of talking to Iraqis, interacting with Iraqis became more and more limited. The problem was not our microphones, the problem was us. It was too dangerous for us to be out in the neighborhoods, and as those times went on, we more and more relied on our Iraqi staff. Ali [Fadhil] worked with us for awhile and we would not have survived without him. They were the ones who went out with the microphones, and still, Iraqis were willing to talk on the record with a microphone.

ANNE GARRELS | NPR

TV tends to—because I think [the military is] not as threatened by the networks or CNN...they get ferried around a lot—Christiane Amanpour comes in and—nothing against Christiane, but she comes in and she gets ferried around; the military are her taxis. She's made the decision and bless her, she's earned it: she's no longer going to cover this on a daily basis, but she comes in, and she and Peter Jennings, when he was alive, they come in and they are ferried around. I mean, Geraldo Rivera, a man who has been excoriated and expelled by the military on several occasions, comes in and nonetheless he gets a Blackhawk as his taxi!

I don't think the newspapers or NPR, who's treated more like a newspaper in many ways, gets that kind of free ride. I don't think that ultimately makes a huge amount of difference to our coverage, but it does show how they really do jump for TV.

The irony, of course, is that TV can't do a really good job in Iraq, because in terms of covering the real Iraqi story—if it is dangerous for the rest of us to go out, for somebody to go out and raise a camera, it is incredibly dangerous. And if Iraqis are afraid of speaking on mike to me, you can imagine how much more frightened they are to show their faces on camera; they're not going to trust the promise that the face will be blacked out or whatever—people are frightened. So I think that TV, pictures, when you can get them, are enormously dramatic, and for the most part I know, watching the networks, they can't do what they'd like to do because people don't want to be seen on camera, or the risk is too great, or they even—I can get out much more, as limited as my access is and as much as I'm using translators as proxies, I still get out all the time. For TV, they're relying almost exclusively on proxies, because of the danger, and it makes it much harder to write a story when you weren't there.

JANE ARRAF | CNN

[One day] the [Iraqi] police came out and they were dragging a suspect out of the car and they started kicking him in the head in front of our cameras and they saw our camera and they just kicked him harder [laughs]. And I said, "Do you really have to kick this guy?" They just kept kicking him. The soldiers came up to us, American soldiers, and tried to take away the tape. That is their automatic reaction—not of senior people but of police and soldiers. We wouldn't give up the tape and we held on to it and after a while we talked to a commanding general who said, "Please don't run that."

I explained that if it happens in front of you and the camera is rolling, I'm really sorry, but that is not negotiable. But what I would do is put it in context, which I did. The context I put it in was that these are Iraqi soldiers and this is the way—on this day in this police station—they were treating suspects that they thought were responsible for killing police officers. This doesn't happen everywhere, but on this day it did. And he was okay with that. And that's the way a lot of them are, and that's why you develop relationships where there is mutual trust. Because at the end of the day when you explain it to them, they get it. They understand that it's not going to do them much good if you agree not to show something because it actually did happen.

MARTIN SMITH | FRONTLINE
I think that—not across the board, not at the highest levels, because the higher you go in the military the more political it gets, until you get to the Chairman of the Joint Chiefs of Staff, who's basically shilling for the administration's policies in many regards, he's appearing on the morning talk shows

on Sundays and protecting the policy—but at the level of the captains and the colonels and some of the generals in the field, these guys are interested in success, and they're interested in their guys living. They're not interested in—spinning doesn't get them anywhere. Many of them we talked to, and it's not always the case, but many of them I thought were really straight-shooters, because the politics and spinning were not of—they were interested in telling you what was going on because they have to honestly assess the situation if they're going to have any success in dealing with it. So if they've got a situation where Kurds and Sunnis and Shia are at each other's throats, they're assessing it honestly, and they share that with you.

In Baqubah we walked in—and this is in 2004, I believe—Baqubah, really hard-hit town, a lot of violence, a lot of bad things are happening there, and a very difficult post, they got fired on a lot. We went into the headquarters of the U.S. command there and talked to a woman about the difficulty of training the police and standing up to Iraqis.

A woman in the military, who was in charge there, she said, "Basically, we're not getting any money. The money is frozen, it's not moving out of Washington, and we're here, it's winter, and the Iraqi police that we're training, equipping, and uniforming don't have jackets, and they're out there freezing." She said it openly. But a lot of times you're informed by what you're told off-camera. And then you can reflect it in the way in which you balance your report. Now you're told by a captain or a colonel what the facts are, and he may not be willing, because he doesn't want to risk his rank and career on going on camera with a complaint, but he can tell you straight out what it is and you can verify it; then you can report it or you can—it changes the way in which you tell your story and how skeptical you are of counterclaims if somebody can lay out the evidence. I found the military very useful in terms of briefings and giving you the straight dope on what was going on.

RAJIV CHANDRASEKARAN |
THE WASHINGTON POST

The soldiers were very edgy. In fact, we were, in those early months, more worried about getting shot at by American forces, because you might come upon a poorly-marked checkpoint or you might stumble upon some forces that had just been attacked and were very itchy with the trigger. In the summer of 2003, we purchased our first armored vehicle, an armored Jeep Cherokee. The rationale was that if you're going to one of those places, you might easily get shot up by either side. It wasn't that we were just concerned about Iraqis, we were worried about American crossfire too. Those were some of the first developments. Then things started to get worse in some of those outlying areas. It became clear that you didn't want to go to some of these places after dark. Even with that, you still got around pretty well through the summer of 2003 and into the fall of 2003.

After it became evident that a lot of contractors were driving around in Jeep Cherokees that looked like ours, I took one and then the second of four SUVs to Sadr City and did the Baghdad equivalent of Pimp My Ride. For sixty bucks, I had it sandblasted and had it painted to look like an Iraqi taxi cab. The really nice paint job on this $90,000 vehicle was stripped off and it was made to look like a ghetto mobile, like a Shiite ghetto mobile from Sadr City.

There came a point through the fall of 2003 when you would stop identifying yourself to strangers as a journalist, as an American journalist. I went through a phase where I would say, I'm an Indian journalist, because I'm of Indian descent even though I was born and raised in California. I used that line, particularly in Fallujah quite a bit. If you were just doing a brief man-on-the-street interview, it was never a big deal. If I were actually sitting down with somebody and doing something substantive, I obviously had to let on who I was. Again, that was also before we learned that the insurgents started using Google to Google people they had captured and figure out who they were.

LUKE BAKER | REUTERS

I frequently went up to Tikrit in the hunt for Saddam. I did it for weeks at a time, embedding with U.S. troops, because everyone had a sense that if he was going to be caught, he was going to be caught around there. It was a pilgrimage for journalists to go up there, and I did it a lot. And I left there, I think I left December 10, 2003. I was due to go on holiday, and there were three of us who went on holiday the same day: the bureau chief, myself, and another guy who was helping out. I was flying to Rome, and the other two guys were flying to London. I landed in Rome and had twenty-six messages on my cell phone. I thought, "That's odd, what's going on?" I got the first one and it was my mother telling me that Saddam had been caught, and I thought, "Good God, I had to find out from my mother that Saddam had been caught. I've just been six weeks with the American military trying to track the guy down."

FARNAZ FASSIHI |
THE WALL STREET JOURNAL

It was on the road to Kirkuk, to Baghdad. The driver said they were kidnappers. And I looked over at this car, right next to me. With five men, with AK-47s out, like, right next to me. This was the summer after the invasion. Right at the beginning. They were shooting. We were flying. That's how fast we were going. We were going really fast. We were in a better car than they were. We were like—hit the ground. We sort of blocked each other's bodies [on the floor of the car]. I don't know how long. But we essentially outraced them. Our car [was] a BMW; I think it was a four-wheel drive. [And the men were in] a white Toyota, I remember. There were like five men. It was very scary. We didn't have a guard; we didn't have a chase car. I kept thinking, "This is it. They're going

to kill us. Take the car. Or kidnap us." Or, as a woman, you're always very aware of rape. Your mind is racing, like, "I can't do this." I just remember thinking, "Oh, my God, this is it."

ALI FADHIL | TRANSLATOR, REPORTER

We were planning to go inside Fallujah [in May 2004] during the war; the plans were to disguise Patrick [Graham] as an Iraqi, as my brother, and try to do a story about the whole situation inside, if we can find a house, decent people who we can trust and stay with them. Of course, there wasn't any other way to go inside other than this; for example, people tried to go with the Red Crescent inside. They were all of them, not kidnapped, but they were jailed in a mosque somewhere and they couldn't do anything.

So what we did is this: we dyed [Graham's] hair. He has yellow hair, so we changed it to black hair. He dressed as an Iraqi, he sat in a car, a normal car, just beside me, and I was driving; we drove inside Fallujah, and that was what we planned. And by the way, we managed to bring for him a fake Iraqi ID that tells that his name is Tariq—his name is Patrick, but we changed it to Tariq…

We felt he should be a mute, and he can't talk. But on the way, we felt they might do something to him and he will talk, so we said let's change it into something else, and because I am a doctor, I said, "Let's change it into that you have a stroke, so you can talk, but you can't talk perfectly." And

Dexter Filkins, a correspondent for
The New York Times, covers the battle
in Falluja in November 2004.
Ashley Gilbertson/Aurora/Getty Images

it happens that he knows a few words, for example, "salaam alaikum" ["peace be with you"] and "shukran" ["thank you"]—that's it. So what we did is we changed it to stroke; I taught him all these symptoms, how to have a stroke, and we went inside.

We had a box full of drugs Patrick brought from a friend, so we said, "We are coming inside, we want to give you drugs, we are caring about the people inside, we are worried about the people getting injured." We crossed like six checkpoints, seven checkpoints. And at the seventh checkpoint people said, "He's your brother?"—I said yes—"What's your name?" I said, "He can't talk properly because he got a stroke." But I don't know why Patrick said, when they asked him his name—he knows [the question] in Arabic "Sheno ismok?" so he answered, "Tariq," and "Tariq" is not the way he should answer [because it is a mispronunciation]. He should have said "Baruk."

And I taught him to say "Baruk," but it was very difficult for him to say it. So he said "Tariq," and they said, "Now he's saying he's your brother and he's saying 'Tariq'? He's a foreigner, he's a spy, come on!" And they took us and they kidnapped us.

It was a checkpoint, and at each checkpoint there are like five, six people, and every checkpoint is like ten meters from the other checkpoint. And you can see the American tanks through the desert, just like two kilometers, one kilometer actually, you can see it. And there was a fight, there was bombing, bullets everywhere, you can

hear it. When we drove, we drove into a dirt road, so the dirt is all over the place, our hair is white—it was very difficult because all the roads were blocked and this was a side road in between the fields. They took us under contract; someone with a rifle was sitting in the back seat, one of them drove my car; I was sitting in the front and Patrick was behind, and they drove us inside the city and they took us to a mosque called the Muhammadiyah Mosque, which was the main headquarters for the insurgency in that war and in the second war as well.

There was the sheikh of the mosque, his name is Dhafir, who now is different: he became anti-insurgents, anti-Americans— he's living in Fallujah under the American notice. They took us inside; there were like people who were—some of them wearing the Islamic dress, some of them were dressed as educated people, like suits, ties, and all of them were very old people except a few people who were doing the serving and holding the prisoners. There was a prison on the second floor of the mosque and we were on the first floor, on the ground floor, and they separated us, me and Patrick—or Tariq at that time. And they asked for his IDs, I gave them his IDs. They took him into one room and I'm in another room; a few minutes later when an investigator came to me, he said, "Why are you lying? He's Spanish." I said, "What, he's Spanish?" He said, "Yes, he spoke to us and he is Spanish." I said, "Well, my brother speaks Spanish"—that's perfect, because I know he's

Canadian, and I know that he won't talk at all, because we agreed that even if we were caught, we'll never say who is he, because this is dangerous, even though he's Canadian and Canada had nothing with the war.

So after I said that, a few minutes later they brought Patrick to me and they apologized for what happened, and they said, "All the city's for you and you can go anywhere under our protection," and they gave us a letter to the fighters, saying to the fighters that they should not stop us doing anything.

So we went around the city, we talked with some of the fighters, we talked to the people. We went actually inside a house who offered for us lunch, so we ate lunch there. And the funny part is in the lunch that Patrick—because I have this humor thing, even in problem situations—Patrick was very hungry and so he was eating and eating until I said, "No, enough." And the people said, "Why? Just leave him to eat. Eat, Tariq, eat." And I said, "He can't eat because he doesn't know when he's going to get full, because he got stroke," and they took the food from him, and in another moment—Tariq, Patrick, he loved drinking tea and smoking a cigarette after lunch—it's like an Iraqi habit—and he loved drinking tea.

When they brought tea for us, they brought one for me and one for Patrick and it was very hot, and I said, "No, no, no, he can't drink tea because it's very hot, he will spill it on himself," and they took the tea from him. At the end, after we finished, after I finished actually, drinking my tea,

I took him to the bathroom to clean his hand, because he had a stroke, and in the bathroom, he punched me, he gave me a blow on my face, and he said, "You fucking asshole, I wanted that tea! I'll kill you after we get out from here!" [laughter].

And after that, we went outside of the city, which was very difficult because the American attack started at the evening, and at one moment my car, I was driving my car, it was like going around itself because we were in the desert and the American tank was firing rockets beside the car because they thought we are insurgents or something. We are three young men inside the car, and finally we found a way—some people helped us to go around, very, very far away towards Yusufiyah—it's even more dangerous than Fallujah—and then we returned to Baghdad in like three hours, which is supposed to be only forty-five minutes or half an hour. The moment we went out of Fallujah, Patrick was sitting behind, he gave me a heavy box on my head from the back and he was shouting in the car, and you can imagine, but it was something. We were very good friends after that.

CHRISTOPHER ALLBRITTON | FREELANCE WRITER

Well, by August [2004] it was very difficult to travel outside of Baghdad, although it wasn't impossible. What we did was we left early in the morning on the day that I went down to Najaf. I pretended to be asleep in the back seat. We had to go through the so-called triangle of death. They were well known to be insurgent towns. We needed to keep a very low profile but the traffic was always really bad going through this little stretch—I just lay down in the back with a kafiyah over my face like I was asleep. And we made it through okay. And once we got to Najaf I felt more endangered by Najaf police than by the Mahdi Army. The Mahdi Army treated me with respect—I'm sure they knew I was an American even though I told them I was Canadian. They all kind of had this look on their face like, "Yeah, Canadian. Whatever you say, buddy."

LIZ SLY | *CHICAGO TRIBUNE*

In the fall of 2004, when the kidnapping started, it became very necessary not to be publicly identified on the streets as a foreigner. I wear a scarf, I wear Iraqi-style clothing. I don't go with the whole abaya [the traditional full-body garment for Islamic women] because I don't walk like I'm an Iraqi that's in an abaya. I'm not that kind of person, but my coloring is very dark and people mistake me for an Iraqi frequently. And if I am your sort of average working woman in Iraqi clothes—that means skirts down to the ankle, a baggy jacket that's long and comes down below your butt, and a plain scarf—people don't give me a second glance. You never talk English on the street; you never take a phone call on the street. For women, in some ways there's a little advantage, because if you are a woman walking with a man, another man, a strange man won't look at her; he can't give her a second glance because it's just not done.

The assumption is this woman is the wife of the guy she is walking with, and you don't look at other people's wives or sisters. At the same time, women don't look around. Women don't catch men's eyes; women keep their eyes on the pavement ahead of them, and walk modestly. And one of the things I've had to learn to do is curb my natural curiosity and instinct to look around me when I'm walking along, which inhibits a little bit of what you can absorb of the scene you're in, which is limiting. My Iraqi staff would say to me, "Stop moving your head, stop looking around!"

YOUSIF MOHAMED BASIL
TRANSLATOR | *TIME* (CNN)

When I want to get from home to my place of work, I'll walk a long distance from my house just not to take a taxi in front of my house. Then I take a taxi, and when I come to the neighborhood where my place of work is, I'll walk from the place where the taxi dropped me for a long distance until I get to the job. Because it's very dangerous to just take off from the taxi in front of your place of work because probably the taxi driver is from your neighborhood or is from a certain group and he might say something bad about you.

PATRICK GRAHAM | FREELANCE WRITER

As a freelance reporter, your driver and translator are your friends, and you pay them badly. And the idea of getting one of them killed seems kind of crazy and not anything I want to have to live with later on. I got a call from one of them yesterday, who's in Fallujah, and I thought he had died. He just disappeared, his e-mail had shut down, and he's a Sunni, a young Sunni man, which is—he'd already been arrested by the Americans and shot at. If the Americans don't get him, there's a good change one of the Shiite militias would have got him. And he phoned to tell me—to make sure that I don't come to Iraq, because he thought it was pointless, especially coming to Fallujah. So a lot of the work I was doing was in Fallujah and Ramadi—it doesn't sound like you can get there unless you're embedded, which is not anything that interested me.

LUKE BAKER | REUTERS

We have a force of about twenty-four Iraqis who are on guard twenty-four hours a day, and then we have three British security advisors. I don't know if that really describes it accurately, but that's kind of what was going on. We've got a hundred and fifteen people working for us in Iraq. We've got a really extensive network of people. About, probably ninety-five of them are locals. Probably a hundred of them are locals. Fifteen of them are foreign journalists and—probably fewer actually, probably about ten at the moment, but in about all, of those hundred and fifteen, seventy are journalists, so thirty-five in Baghdad and about thirty-five spread about the country—stringers. We cover eighteen cities across the country. So those guys are, in a lot of respects, our eyes and ears on the ground.

GHAITH ABDUL-AHAD | *THE GUARDIAN*, GETTY IMAGES

I studied architecture in Baghdad and I was always interested in photography. In 2000, 2001, I was walking around Baghdad taking pictures and documenting, kind of from an architectural point of view, Baghdad's traditions and how things were. And then the war happened, and I was shooting during the war, I was shooting film, just shooting for myself, and I had become very interested in how Baghdad was changing—buildings were being bombed, streets were changing, people were packing and leaving. Just doing this as an inside point of view of Baghdad.

Then three days before the end of the war I was arrested by a Republican Guard unit. Stupidly I was on a bicycle in Baghdad during the war with a backpack on my back, and they stopped me, opened the backpack, and saw two cameras, film, shortwave radio, and English notes, so—obviously a spy—and about six hours after that they kept trying to know when I had parachuted in. And at that point I had spent almost five years and a half running away from military service and I was always kind of hiding in Iraq all the time. I didn't have any ID cards or anything, and then they put me in front of a tree, they were trying to shoot me, and then they decided to question me further. They took me to a room where I managed to bribe the officer and he let me go.

Three days after that, the Americans came to Baghdad and out of curiosity I just really wanted to see Saddam's palace. So I walked, winding my way through American checkpoints, claiming that I was a British journalist and saying that I lost my ID card. And I went into the presidential palace and I was given an official tour by one American soider as a British journalist. That was in Baghdad, tenth of April 2003. And at the end of that day I started working as a journalist. I was trying to hitch a ride and I stumbled on journalists and I was hired by British journalists who were with *The Guardian* and I developed this relationship with *The Guardian.* Then I left *The Guardian*, went to *The New York Times* and worked there as a news assistant for eight or nine months and then went to Reuters. I had three or four months training working for Reuters and then left Reuters and started freelancing as a photographer…

I did grow up in Iraq, but I grew up in such a way that I'm almost an outsider. I don't have a big tribe. I don't have a big huge history, I'm not handicapped by all the tribal family beliefs and religious traditions that will connect me to Iraq. So it's a funny thing, I grew up in Iraq but I am considered an outsider, I will always be considered an outsider inside my community and society. Sometimes it's a handicap to be an Iraqi inside Iraq, especially in these circumstances. You want to do a story and the people will be very suspicious of you, an Iraqi without tribal connection. Sometimes it's better to be an outsider, they will talk more freely to you as an outsider sometimes. But again, it's an amazing privilege to be, and so spoiling, to

be walking in a place, a very difficult place, a very hard story, but still feel that you can have extra points because you look like an Iraqi, you talk like an Iraqi.

You have extra breathing space as an Iraqi, you speak the language, you speak the accent, everything's fine. So as long as you are traveling in your car, you're fine, as long as you are walking in the streets, you're fine. The moment you carry a camera out, the moment you pull out a notebook, the moment you stay and show that you are a journalist, all the breathing space you can have as an Iraqi disappears and you become a journalist. And maybe for a westerner they will have the privilege of being kidnapped for two, three months, while an Iraqi will just be killed and considered a collaborator or a spy. So the two inches of breathing space is very useful for doing your research, but the moment you want to shoot a photo, or the moment you want to do your actual story, you fall under the category of journalist, who are all targets. And being in Iraq for a long period of time, and going around the street and covering the events, people know you as a journalist, so you have this profile as a journalist. And once you go somewhere else—"Oh, here is the journalist"—and again, you lose your two inches of breathing space.

HANNAH ALLAM | KNIGHT RIDDER (McCLATCHY)

Yasser [Salihi, a stringer] was an amazing journalist, a very dear friend. He was beloved by every single reporter who came in and we got to a point where we had competing demands where, "If I'm coming, I'm working with Yasser." Everybody wanted to work with him because he's just this bright spot. He was wonderful, talented, fair, committed, just every adjective you can think of, a great guy. And he and I had been in insurgent-controlled Fallujah together. He and I had gone there a lot together. I mean, just the most crazy harebrained dangerous things you can think of. And then [in November 2004], he was killed on his day off.

He was in his neighborhood, and it is predominantly a Sunni neighborhood. It's known for being fairly anti-American, lot of attacks there. And he was just on his way to buy some gas to take his little daughter to the swimming pool, like he'd promised her for a long time, and he drove too close to a U.S. checkpoint that was unmarked and not a usual checkpoint—it was one of those that would spring up overnight—and he was shot once by a U.S. sniper. He was shot in the head.

TOM LASSETER | KNIGHT RIDDER (McCLATCHY)
We got a copy of [the U.S. Army] report [of the Salihi shooting]. They ended up giving us their full—I forget the designation of these reports, but they gave us the entire copy of it, which doesn't always happen. And I spent a lot of time campaigning for that, to get a copy, to be able to give to his family. I didn't know that they would like what it said, but at least it was doing something. And

the report found that the sniper was acting within the rules of engagement. The report found that Yasser was a short distance from the checkpoint and at a high rate of speed and they feared he was a car bomber. So that's what happened.

ALISSA RUBIN | *LOS ANGELES TIMES*
For senior reporters who have worked in war zones, there's a kind of, you know, checklist of things you need to know, and we're much more attuned to what those are. And the editors are, too: Well, do you know that you can go there? Has anyone else gone there yet? Was there fighting there recently? Have there been kidnappings? Are other news organizations using armored cars? Do you want to use local guards? How many local guards do you think you'd need? Not traveling with local guards in the same car you're in, so you know, if shooting starts, they're not shooting out of your car and people aren't shooting into your car. I mean, these become second nature.

PATRICK COCKBURN | *THE INDEPENDENT* (LONDON)
One has to spend an enormous amount of time thinking about one's own security, but often doing very boring things, like making sure that the driver's checked the tires properly, or where did they get the gasoline from, because a lot of black-market gasoline is watered down. It's extremely dangerous for the car to break down in some neighborhood of Baghdad and it could be fatal. There are a lot of very boring things

The bodies of Iraqi civilians lie outside a
morgue in Baghdad after at least thirty-four
people, mostly young men seeking to join the
Iraqi army, were killed in a spate of suicide
bombings. July 10, 2005. Yuri Kozyrev

that could happen that one should really check about and often journalists don't.

JAMES HIDER | *THE TIMES* (LONDON)

By early 2005—as you know I've got brown hair—by this time I had dyed my hair and eyebrows black, as an attempt to look slightly less foreign. I just did it myself. It was a disaster—my hair turned blue so I had to do it again. I looked like a complete freak. Then once I got it right, I looked like a very sick Kurdish person who was having a rough time, which, you know, lots of Iraqis don't look in great shape either. It really worked quite well. I mean, some people actually spoke to me in Arabic when I had black hair. I felt like I looked like Roy Orbison's ghost, but people would ask me stuff in Arabic.

I started to get some Iraqi clothes, some horrible nylon clothes and some jeans that came practically up to my chest, and cheap Iraqi shoes. I stopped carrying my stuff in a western-style bag. I put my stuff in a plastic bag with a Coke bottle, and had my tape recorder and my note pad in there. Eventually I developed this whole thing so that I could get around. If we got caught in traffic I'd hold up an Iraqi newspaper and pretend I was reading it so that nobody could see my face.

And I remember one time, I was in the car, and I was sitting in the back and the driver was up in front. We stopped at a junction quite close to a hotel. And there was this little girl hawking sweets in the street, and I was talking to my driver at the moment she stuck her head in my window. We were

talking in English, and she rushed to the car behind and started shouting, "Amreeki, Amreeki," and I don't know if she was told to do that if something happened or if she was just freaked out by foreigners. Luckily, the car behind was my chase car, and so Yasser, who is my chase-car driver, got on the walkie-talkie to my driver and said, "This girl is telling everyone that you're American, get out of there quickly." So my driver just jumped the junction and we got back. But it was one of those things where you think, "God, everyone's watching." You know you could be tricked into being revealed for who you are by some six-year-old girl who's selling candy in the street. And so you just have to be so careful, and even with disguises it's still incredibly dangerous, and you know, it's getting worse.

CHRISTOPHER ALLBRITTON | FREELANCE WRITER

I was still going out probably until midsummer 2005. I cut back on it, but I was still going out. By the middle of summer 2005 I would go out rarely and it was only to go to set interviews. Because I cannot pass at all; I don't speak Arabic, I don't look Arabic. If anyone sees me they're going to obviously tell I was a foreigner so I had to curtail my movements. By fall 2005 it was embeds and just going to government offices. I couldn't get out. I couldn't go to the market. I couldn't go get a feel for the city. I couldn't really breathe the story anymore of what was happening to Iraqis. And at that time I decided if I can't do this then there really is no point in being here. I didn't want to keep sending Iraqi stringers and keep doing this by remote control. I went back and forth because I was really committed to the story.

BORZOU DARAGAHI | *LOS ANGELES TIMES*
Another strategy I have is I'll go to the scene of the car bombing and I'll collect cell-phone numbers from people there and then quickly go, within like ten or fifteen minutes, and then call them and get their accounts as I'm driving back.

RICHARD ENGEL | **NBC NEWS**
[My Arabic is] a little confused now. By now it's become fairly Iraqi, because most of the people I speak to now in Arabic are in Iraq. So it's become confusing; if I'm speaking to someone on the phone, they won't know where I'm from. They'll be confused. They'll know that I'm not Iraqi, but they don't really know. Who's this guy? Is he a Lebanese guy? Is he a Syrian guy? Who is this person? It's confusing. So, that can also be to my advantage. The Arabic has been—during the days of Saddam it was a problem. They didn't like the fact that I spoke Arabic. It made me much more dangerous to them. And it was a problem—generally the minder acted as a translator, so I didn't need that, my minder was just a chaperone. And I had little tricks: I used to find the big and fat minders and then walk them all day long. Just walk them, you know? I never took taxis, just walked. It was a trick of an Italian journalist, friend of mine, he's a triathlete, and he used to walk his minders miles, until they just drop and

say, we'll just see you later. So there were stupid little games like that we would play, and then later on, sure if you speak Arabic you can go to people's houses, you sit down with them and you can talk with them. It's not just speaking Arabic, it's the gestures, it's the religious references, it's the sense of humor, it's the old—we can talk about movies, old Egyptian movies that we've both seen. When they're talking about some sort of Egyptian pop star I know who they're talking about, so it's not just the language, it's knowing the culture and their terms of reference.

So I think without speaking the language, it's hard to make any kind of connection with someone who then will open up to you and trust you. I have people that I consider very close friends in the country. And now it's even more vital because our movements are so limited; I spend half the day on the phone, ah, I spend all day on the phone. I'm in touch with people in Samara, in Basra, in Fallujah—none of them speak English. Without Arabic, I don't know how I would be able to do my job: I'm all day long speaking to people all around the country who don't speak English.

THANASSIS CAMBANIS |
THE BOSTON GLOBE
I think no reporting of note would be getting done inside of Iraq without the local staff of the journalistic community, and it's probably a unique phenomena in war reporting because there wasn't really a developed reliable local media in Iraq the way there

was, say, in the Balkans when the war there started. And at the same time, organizations came in with a lot of resources and a lot of money and had a year of free-reign reporting, so what happened is people hired smart Iraqis as translators and then worked with them really intensely for a year more in a reporter-translator relationship, and then, once security constraints kicked in, were able to turn to the translators that they knew well, trusted, and promote them to reporters, effectively. That's what happened. And as it became more and more constricted, more and more of the reporting has become the product of our Iraqi colleagues, and in a lot of places it really is an equal colleague relationship.

Newspapers are functioning in much the same manner as a wire service bureau in terms of how they work, not in terms of what they produce. Outside of Baghdad you have a network of stringers who phone in reports and check things that you hear about. You know, you hear from the U.S. military that a bomb went off, so you have your local stringer go to the morgue and interview the local. And inside Baghdad it's the local staff who are really telling the reporters what's happening, particularly in the neighborhoods we never go into, like the Sunni neighborhoods. Towards the end of my time there [in early 2006], we had our local guys doing a lot of our interviews and the reporting for us as well. The typical mix on a double-byline story would be that I would do one or two long interviews in a safe place—somebody's home or in a hotel

lobby—and then our translator would go out to get color from a neighborhood I couldn't get into. Or didn't feel comfortable getting into. So these stories were at least half and half, but the half that the local staff was providing was the half which without the story couldn't exist.

LARRY KAPLOW | COX NEWSPAPERS
I've been working with the same main translator for more than a year and another one for, I guess, almost a year, and they know that if they make a mistake I can get fired. And I tell them over and over, "Look, if you can't get it, tell me. That's all right. I just need to know that I'm not saying anything more than you actually got out on the street and you're not putting words in these people's mouths." You ask them a lot of questions about where did you talk to the guy, what did he look like. And sometimes you often ask them to get [phone] numbers, so you can have them or another translator call the people back and ask them questions. It's not because they would purposely try to mislead me, although some translators would do that, too, but because they might make assumptions that are not acceptable assumptions for American newspapers to make. Or they might have planted the idea with someone and just got an affirmative response that they then embellished with their own assumptions of what that person is trying to say. And there is just so much bad information here. You just have to check and check and check things over and over and over. People will pass on apocryphal stories

as if they happened to them personally. And you find out, well, no, it was actually a cousin; well, no, it wasn't a cousin. Well, no, actually it didn't quite happen like that anyway.

ALI FADHIL | TRANSLATOR, REPORTER

You remember Miss Jill Carroll? She was kidnapped on the seventh of January [2006]. On the eighth—actually the same night, on the seventh—midnight, twelve-thirty, my house was raided by special forces, American forces, and they thought Jill Carroll was in my house. They brought a picture of her and said, "She's at this house; where is she?"

What happened is they used explosives to open the three doors of the house; every single window of the house was blown up, and in seconds. We thought that a plane maybe fell down on top of the house—we were sleeping: me and my wife, Zina, and two kids, Adam and Sarah. Suddenly we heard this explosion, woke up; Sarah was still sleepy, and in seconds the door was opened—the room door—and a rifle came through and shot bullets inside the room while we are asleep. And I thought, "This is a gang"; that's what I thought, and I throw myself on Zina and the kids. They woke up, they were crying, and in seconds American soldiers are surrounding my bed while I am sleeping with my wife and two kids, and they took me down from the bed. Zina was crying and shouting, Sarah as well; Adam was crying—he was just eight months by that time.

They took me downstairs. In a moment they beat me—just one soldier—and in another moment they brought a dog who started barking at me, and then a captain came and questioned me—showed the pictures, he didn't say the name, just showed the pictures. "This woman is in your house." "No." And he said, "This is Mashhadani house," by which he means this is a Sunni house; Mashhadani is a Sunni name, a Sunni tribe name. I said, "This can't be—go to the hall, you'll see a big picture of Imam Ali"—this is a shrine, it's a figure of the Shiites. And he went to the hall and he came back, said then, "Who are you? Are you a journalist, as you said?" I said, "Yes, I'm a journalist, filmmaker, working for the British media, blah, blah." It didn't help at the beginning; minutes later, he brought out a camera which I use, and it happened that in that camera there was a mini-DVD tape that shows the Green Zone, and I'm standing in front of the camera talking about the Green Zone, how at one time the Green Zone was the place where the CPA ran Iraq, because I was doing at that time a thing about the reconstruction in Iraq. And he said, "Why do you have these tapes?" I said, "Because I'm a filmmaker and we were doing this project"; I was still doing this project. He said, "Do you realize that these places were targeted two days ago?" I said, "No way, because two days ago I was inside the Green Zone, filming from inside the Green Zone." Later on, he came back with another captain, another officer, and he said, "It seems like there is a mistake, but we want to take you to a place to interrogate you, and you might help us in helping this lady, but we have to take you now and release you tomorrow morning—we promise." And I said, "I have no problem if you are taking me alone and not taking my brother-in-law or my father-in-law."

And by the way, they beat my father-in-law, they beat my brother-in-law a lot, and they were really, really humiliated—more than me; later on, when they knew I was a journalist, I was treated like a prince. They blindfolded me, they put me in an armored vehicle. And finally I found myself in a room, a small room with wooden walls, a table in the middle, a mattress at the side of the wall, and a very, very young American soldier with a pistol attached to his leg, standing there guarding me. And minutes later, two American civilians came into the room. They asked me, "Mr. Fadhil, do you know why you're here?" I said, "Yes, to interrogate me." They said, "No, it's because there was a mistake, and we apologize for what happened." At that moment I was—it's a shock, because they threw the furniture all over the house, they destroyed the entrances of the house. My daughter was shocked— now she hates Americans. She doesn't want to believe that she's in America. She's three years old, and if you tell her you're in America, she's gonna shout. [Fadhil is now living in New York City.]

They said, "In the morning we will release you as soon as possible." I said, "What about the compensation?" And they said, "In the morning, sure, people will come and bring the compensation, and we'll talk with you about the compensation." In the

morning, two American civilians—different civilians—came in. They were like people working for the private security forces. They said, "We're gonna drive you now out of the place, with blindfolded eyes, and we brought the compensations." They had two envelopes; they opened the first one and they said, "This is a thousand dollars for the damages of the house." And they opened the other, "This is five hundred for the time you spent with us in the Green Zone," which was the highest-ever salary I ever got in my entire life. I didn't say anything, I just wanted to get out, and they took me in a car and drove right and left, right and left, for like minutes, and then I found myself in a place between concrete barricades. When I walked out from the place a few meters, I found myself in the worst place I would ever imagine myself in. It was the south gate of the Green Zone. That is the place where many car bombs happened, and if someone walks like how I walk, with civilian clothes outside of the Green Zone, and my face is not washed and my hair like this, and I walked out with money, with a thousand, five hundred dollars in my pocket, and the insurgents caught me—it's no way. Thank God, it was easy to get a taxi. I found the whole house was worse than what I thought: everything was destroyed—all the rooms were ruined, most of the furniture was broken.

LUKE BAKER | REUTERS
We've had four [staff members] killed, three of whom have been killed by the U.S. military [Waled Khaled, Mazen Dana,

Taras Protsyuk]; the fourth [Dhia Najim] is under investigation. We've asked for further investigation; as far as we understand he was wearing press credentials—a helmet, a flak jacket with "press" on it—and filming U.S. military operations in Ramadi, and he was shot in the back of the head.

And what we've tended to find in any of these investigations to do with [Khaled, Dada, Protsyuk, and Najim]—what we've found, generally speaking, is that the initial report has tried to approximate the events that led up to the incident and how it occurred, with statements from the soldiers who were present, who all sort of corroborate one another's stories—from our point of view, often almost too precisely. Or they're so riddled with inconsistencies and errors that it makes you wonder why on earth the person who was compiling the information didn't go back and ask more questions, because it was either too neat or so untidy, so error-ridden that it makes you wonder whether any investigation had gone on.

FARNAZ FASSIHI |
THE WALL STREET JOURNAL

We all have a team of Iraqi staff whose lives we've seen unfold for three years before our eyes. We know their families; we know what's happening to their extended families. We live in a hotel, the Hamra Hotel. The receptionist, one receptionist, his house was bombed. The other receptionist in building two, his only son was kidnapped because he was selling SIM cards ["smart cards" for

mobile phones] and they thought he was selling SIM cards to Americans. And got killed in front of their eyes. We are living through their eyes—through our daily contact, with the house boy, the guard. And our job, by definition, means we spend hours and hours talking to people about their experiences. We don't just say, "Hi, how are you? What's going on outside?" We sit them down and spend two hours and say, "What's going on in your neighborhood? What's going on with your cousin?"

RICHARD ENGEL | NBC NEWS
There was the attack on the Golden Dome Mosque in Samarra [on February 22, 2006] and Al-Arabiyah dispatched a crew up there—chased the story, big story, one of the most holy [Shia] shrines in the world, certainly in Iraq, is badly damaged, if not destroyed. People are livid—this is a sensitive time to do such a sensitive attack. Al-Arabiyah, like you'd cover a fire or breaking news, they pack up a crew and they send them off from Baghdad to go cover the story. Well, it didn't go particularly well. They were stopped. The correspondent was taken out of the car, executed. Her crew was taken out of the car and executed. And that was her local crew.

So that is the reality of chasing a breaking news story. So you can't really do it. You have to rely on someone who's from there, who's bringing you the tapes, and then you have to piece together what happened from accounts from the military, accounts from eyewitnesses, accounts from hospital figures,

all of whom maybe have credibility problems.
You have to piece together the best you can
to come up with a mosaic of what's going on.
That's the reality of it. It's not easy because if
you get a crew and chase this breaking news
story, you might not come back.

IX

THE GOOD NEWS

ANTHONY SHADID |
THE WASHINGTON POST
In October 2003, I think that was when
the first salvo in this good news, bad
news debate started going on. And I
started questioning myself. I had just
been in the States for a couple of weeks.
I remember coming back to Baghdad. It
was a quiet day. The weather was nice and
it put me in a certain mood. And I may
have been intimidated a little bit by this
notion of good news and bad news. And
I started questioning my own reading of
the situation. Am I getting it wrong? Am
I not understanding what's happening?
Maybe it is better than I think it is. And I
remember writing a story, and I think the
story reflected that—what's the word I want
to use?—I think that story reflected my

internal questioning more than it should
have. And I think it reflected less than what
I was actually seeing on the ground. And
I regret that story, that's one of the stories
that I count as a mistake that I did in my
time there. But it came out of that thing of,
again, not sticking to what you're hearing,
not sticking to what you're seeing, and kind
of listening to these—what are to me, when
you get down to it—these kind of mindless
debates over what news should be.

PATRICK GRAHAM | **FREELANCE WRITER**
A friend of mine who was working for a
British paper kept getting a lot of pressure
to write "good-news" stories. I can remember
him saying, "I've written a good-news story
in Hillah; I hope they print it before Hillah
blows up."

RAJIV CHANDRASEKARAN |
THE WASHINGTON POST

You've got journalists saying to the embassy there, "So tell us about the reconstruction projects you're doing, tell us about the great things you're doing so we can write about it and show this side of the story." You've got public information officers saying, "Sure, we'll take you there, but you can't say where it is, and you can't name anybody, and you can't take any pictures, because if we point out the location of this, it could be a target for the insurgency, and if we name people, they could be subject to retribution." Is that really progress when you can't go and report basic facts of something because they're too worried it's going to be attacked?

YOUSIF MOHAMED BASIL | TRANSLATOR
TIME (CNN)

As an Iraqi, living inside Iraq, I cannot hear good news, and even if there is good news, you cannot hear it with the noises of explosions and the noises of the terrorists and the noises of American military operations. It's very difficult to hear a lot of things. It's very difficult to practice a lot of rights. It's very difficult to practice freedom. It's very difficult to do a lot of things. So, there's no good news about Iraq. There's no good news at all.

GHAITH ABDUL-AHAD |
THE GUARDIAN, GETTY IMAGES

I've had people tell me when you go to car bomb scenes, try to take these pictures that suggest the scene without really showing the goriness of the scene. But I'm sorry, what do I do, just turn around and take a picture of the crying woman instead of taking the pictures of the dying bodies? Again, I feel very strongly about this thing, people should see, people should realize, it's really ugly out there. And you should see it. You can't censor reality, you can't censor the war, you can't be always sensitive to the feelings of your readers, because it's reality.

We are trying to cover the realities, and sometimes I think, I strongly believe, that because of the security situations in Iraq, because some of us are really jaded, we are not actually conveying how horrible the situation is on the ground. I mean, I can agree with the debate that we are not getting the full picture, because the full picture is so...bad in Iraq. And still reading newspapers you get A, B, and C is bad and D and E is good, so this is kind of balanced reporting. It almost reaches this point where there is nothing good. I mean, what, kids are going to the school. But kids used to go to the school before the war. Electricity? Getting two hours of electricity instead of one hour? It's absurd, this whole debate about good news vs. bad news is absurd. What's happening in Iraq is really bad, and I'm not defending Iraq, I'm not saying Iraq's really bad because of the war, that Iraq was really beautiful before the war, because that's another absurd debate, as if the Iraqis can't get anything between a dictatorship or 150,000 U.S. troops on the ground and the realities of war. This whole debate of Iraq under Saddam, Iraq under the Americans, both are bad and we should find a solution in the middle.

So this debate accusing the media of not conveying the good news is such a—I mean do those people know what we are digging through when we go to Iraq? Just flying into Baghdad, driving, just doing the simplest, the basic, simple things, just being in Baghdad, existing in Baghdad is one of the most dangerous things you can do in your life, let alone covering it. So the effort we put into writing a story, any simple story, is enormous. And none of us, I don't know any journalist who accepts taking such a risk just to manipulate the truth or write the bad news because you have this hidden agenda. People are getting killed on a sectarian basis, people are leaving their neighborhoods, the lines are there. Militias are roaming the streets, despots are functioning in Iraq. People are getting kidnapped, people are getting killed. Everyone's getting killed: barbers, professors, officers, insurgents, Americans, everyone's getting killed. So what are you going to write? And then, when there is good news in Iraq, we do write about these things, such as the elections. We all wrote about the elections, every journalist and photographer went to Iraq to cover the elections. And the elections were good news...at least for two days.

BORZOU DARAGAHI | *LOS ANGELES TIMES*

They would spend ridiculous amounts of money on painting schools and, you know, hire some fancy contractor to paint the

schools as opposed to giving some Iraqis the job. So there were a lot of complications with the reconstruction. Everyone was trying to make a buck or two off this thing—and it was wrong! It was wrong! It didn't work! All these theories [Secretary of Defense Donald] Rumsfeld had about this leaner, meaner military that subcontracts everything—it just didn't work. It was a failure. You can say that objectively.

CAROLINE HAWLEY | BBC

I'll never forget going to a school that was supposedly rehabilitated. And there was the adviser of the Education Ministry and he was literally, virtually in tears because of the shoddy job that had been done. It was basically a paint job had been done in the school; it hadn't really been renovated. The toilets didn't work, and this was the school that we had been taken to kind of showcase the reconstruction at the beginning of the school year. And it was clear that the contract to do the school had passed through many hands, and a very cheap job had been done at the end.

LARRY KAPLOW | COX NEWSPAPERS

You will find people [among U.S. military and embassy officials in Baghdad] who will talk frankly to you, but the question is what they know.

They may be telling you the truth, that this project they're working on or this new initiative they're undergoing, is a good idea that's worked in other places, and the Iraqis

A U.S. Army captain lies dead on the kitchen floor of a house in Fallujah that had been used as a base by insurgents. He was shot by insurgents as he entered. (This photo did not appear in any mainstream U.S. newspapers except in a handful of stories about self-censorship.) November 13, 2004. Stefan Zaklin/European Pressphoto Agency

they're working on it with tell them really good things about how much they like it. That might all be true, and from their point of view totally frank, but it might not have any significance for the broader picture in Iraq.

Like the school work that Bechtel was doing at the beginning. To their eyes, they were going out and giving contractors money to work on hundreds of schools around the country, and then when we went out to look at them the principals of these schools would say, "Well, I didn't even know about it, and some guys came, Iraqi contractors, and said they had to renovate the school, and they took out all the ceiling fans, which were really good ones, and replaced them with really cheap ones, and took out our floor tiles, I guess to resell them, and replaced them with cheaper tiles. And the school basically has a new coat of paint and we still don't have running water in the bathrooms, and there's still sewage piling up outside." And the Americans who were telling me about it actually thought these projects were coming off all right, and they weren't. And they certainly weren't having the overall effect that they were intending to have, which was to build confidence in the American administration, and subsequently the Iraqi government, among only the Iraqi people.

Another example would be the water systems. We kept hearing about the water system in Sadr City and how the army was spending all this money to put down new water lines. And they did that, but the overall water system in Baghdad was so neglected and weak that they couldn't get enough water to these new power lines. So people in the first house on the block would get it in their sink. The people in the middle of the block wouldn't have enough pressure even to get it to their sink; they would take it out of a little pipe at ground level. And the people at the end of the block wouldn't get anything, and then a new line would feed the beginning of the block. And I talked to both Americans and the city of Baghdad water people about it, and they said, "Well, yeah, that's true. It's just such an overwhelming mess, that we do all of this and it still doesn't have a huge impact, a big impact for actual people receiving the water."

DAN MURPHY |
THE CHRISTIAN SCIENCE MONITOR

Good news? My first inclination is to say, "What fucking good news?" The violence and criminality of Iraq has only grown in the three years that I've been here. And there is not an honest metric that shows anything but that. That's the big story.

If the Jets and the Sharks were ruling the streets of Manhattan after dark, that's the big story, not whether or not the municipality painted a few schools. Now, we have covered in great length and detail, and I'm talking about the press in general, all sorts of stuff that's been done, whether it's been power plants that have been redone, water plants that have been rebuilt. Of course, after a while the Americans didn't want you to go see stuff they'd rebuilt because if it gets publicized, it's more likely to get blown up sooner. Reconstruction has failed because there is a war on. And I'm not aware of any single war in human history in which basic living conditions of citizens living in the war zone improved before the war ended.

THANASSIS CAMBANIS |
THE BOSTON GLOBE

That's a debate I don't like to get drawn into because I think the terms are phony. It's a fake question that's designed by people who want a specific answer. It's not a question that is ever asked by people who are seriously interested in understanding what's happening, and the terms of it—"good news, bad news," kind of like "good guys, bad guys"—connotes such a Manichaean and simplistic view of the world as to be very uncurious. That being said, again, anyone who's actually interested in seeing what's going on in Iraq and assessing our work there would actually look at our clips. Whenever people would confront me with that I would say, "LexisNexis me first, see what I wrote and then if you still think that's a question we'll talk about it." The people who asked me that question were people who didn't read the newspaper, and if I engaged them they would usually end up apologizing because it would outrage me. I'd say, "Hey what's most important in people's lives when they're getting killed on the way to the grocery store isn't that the grocery store has a greater selection of imported cookies

than it did before."

LIZ SLY | CHICAGO TRIBUNE

I think of it in terms of a cancer patient who's terminally ill and they shed a few pounds they need to lose because of their illness, and what's the headline here, what's the real story? The fact is this patient is dying, he's really sick, and the fact that they've got their ingrown toenail repaired at the same time isn't really the point.

SCOTT PETERSON |
THE CHRISTIAN SCIENCE MONITOR

There was another big report about a gang rape in which two girls had basically been picked up by American military forces and dropped off the next day. One of them died in the hospital the next day from wounds, and the second one was killed by her family because she had been so defiled. And this was a horrific story that appeared on the front of one of the Iraqi newspapers. And of course, the newspaper eventually, when this was all found to be completely fabricated, they ran a little correction saying "That wasn't true." But you know, there were still [some] seventeen thousand front pages out there, in Baghdad and elsewhere, that had this story running, and that was picked up by a lot of other news organizations without checking, and people believed it.

But those are the kind of things that shape people's perception, but it almost gets, in a sense, when you ask a question about what hope, or what positive things were there, there was so much chaos, and people, as these kind of stories came out, began to believe some of the most horrific and salacious stories about how occupation forces, you know the Americans and others, were dealing with the Iraqis, to the point where you really couldn't, where really it was a no-win game in terms of what the Americans were doing. I mean they just couldn't win. So, in other words, if they were busy painting schools one place, then just down the street where something else happened, they were being accused of or blamed for something else. And of course, it didn't take much to allow Iraqis to do that, because there were also very real stories of American abuses and heavy handedness and things like that which then just helped a lot of people reinforce those views, and then believe much more deeply the worst stories you could imagine.

ANDREW LEE BUTTERS | FREELANCE WRITER
I think a good question is how accurate a picture of Iraq Americans actually want. When I came home to the United States in fall 2004, around the time of the elections, people would ask me about Iraq at every party or event. I remember being at a Republican election-night party in Delaware, because my uncle was running for governor of Delaware, and people just asked me about Iraq. They couldn't understand and were just very surprised to hear me say that things weren't actually going very well. Somehow they would see these explosions and just think that it's okay when things just blew up

all the time. Somehow—as these bombings keep going on—there was a flourishing civil society going on? A society that just ignores these things? Much responsibility is placed on the press, what they're doing and what they're not doing. But I think the American public shared a certain amount of responsibility by shutting its eyes.

ANTHONY SHADID |
THE WASHINGTON POST
When I hear this term "good news," I think of the Arab world I used to cover in 1995, official news agencies, writing about the accomplishments of President Mubarak. I mean, it was despicable. This was good news in their eyes. I just don't understand the distinction [between "good" stories and "bad" ones]. I mean, what Iraq is today and what they envisioned it being before the invasion of 2003—how else do you chronicle that except through the deterioration of the country? It's not a success story, and to call it a success story is propagandistic at this point.

DEXTER FILKINS | THE NEW YORK TIMES
What has struck me about the criticism about us, about the press in this war, is, number one, how virulent it is, absolutely take-no-prisoners, the "you're not an American and I hope you die" sort of criticism. But it's being made by people who aren't there and who claim some kind of superior knowledge even though they're not there. I remember when I was in Fallujah, I was with a company of soldiers when the marines invaded

Fallujah to take it back from the insurgents in November 2004. We went into that city on foot. I was with those guys for eight days, and a quarter of the unit was killed or wounded, I mean it was an absolute bloodbath. But I was there, and on one or two occasions I was able to hook up my satellite phone and I downloaded some stuff, hoping to get some stuff from my office in New York. I remember there were people sending e-mails to me in the United States telling me that I was out of my mind about what I was seeing and that I was wrong. Maybe I was wrong, but I mean how would somebody in Minnesota who is sitting at their computer screen . . . but anyway, that's the world that we live in.

JON LEE ANDERSON | *THE NEW YORKER*
I remember—September 2004, I think it was. Everybody was commenting on Farnaz Fassihi's e-mail [about living and reporting in a deteriorating Iraq, which Fassihi had sent to friends in September 2004 and ended up circulating on the Internet], in which she expressed just what it was like to report in Iraq, sort of no-holds barred, and I happened to be on book tour in the United States following that, and everybody was talking about it—all the editors. And I think it made a lot of people stop and think, "Well, how come everybody's so surprised about this? We thought they knew."

I am in a lot of my pieces where it seemed necessary to be so, where if things happened to me or I witnessed them, they're in the pieces—but that isn't necessarily the case for a lot of newspaper reporters. They're more confined to reporting what their assigned news assignment or the perceived news of the day is. And I think that particularly made a lot of newspaper reporters stop and think, "Well, why is everybody so surprised?"

JOHN BURNS | *THE NEW YORK TIMES*
I thought that [Farnaz Fassihi's] e-mail was very damaging and, frankly, untrue. And it was untrue even of Farnaz's own journalism because she was a brave and resourceful reporter herself. But it encouraged the view that there was nothing that could be done usefully and that we were locked up in our compound. And it just wasn't true.

Those people who are looking for a way to discredit us—I think more from the left than the right, actually—people who think this war was fatally conceived and was doomed to failure of course have an interest in representing the press as having undercovered all the things that have gone wrong. And those people latched on to [Farnaz's] e-mail in the aftermath to say, "Well, of course, we're not in a position to tell the truth about Iraq." It's simply not true.

When this crops up in my e-mail, as it does often enough, from people who haven't taken the trouble to read *The New York Times*, saying, "You never cover this, you never cover that," I think, "Look, first, if you read the paper, you'll find that we do cover these things. And secondly, come on out here and spend a few days with us and see how difficult this is. How we do actually go out and take enormous risks." My problem with our staff is not getting them to go out. It's cautioning them that if we're going to stay in business, if we're going to stay alive, we have to be pretty shrewd about the risks that we take.

DEXTER FILKINS | *THE NEW YORK TIMES*

There's a constant everyday temptation to answer the question whether this gigantic, unbelievably ambitious undertaking that is the constructing of a democracy in Iraq is going to succeed or fail. And I know I ask myself that question every day when I'm there: Is it failing or is it succeeding? I always ask myself that question, and it certainly informs everything I do: Where's it headed? Is it going down or is it going up? But I would say that I think that's something that we should always be thinking about, and I think it's something that I hope our readers think about a lot as well. But I'd also say that we're not, and we shouldn't be expected to be in the business of predicting how things are going. And there's a temptation to do that, and there are recriminations or criticisms that we've faced because we've not done that. "Why didn't you tell us that this was going to fail?" etcetera, etcetera. So I guess I would say—and I don't care, you don't even have to print this—that our job is, first, to report what happens, and what happened that day, why and how and all that. But it's not really our job to guess what's going to come next, and I think that in the sort of supercharged atmosphere that we're in over this war, because it's been

so polarizing, there is a temptation and an expectation by many people that we do that, and I think it's important that we don't. And I don't think it's appropriate. It's not appropriate that people would expect that we would, you know?

LARRY KAPLOW | COX NEWSPAPERS

I don't go out saying today I'm going to do a negative story, I'm going to do a positive story. I go out everyday and try to think of what are the things I can get my notebook around that reflect what I think is going on here in a bigger picture. And that might be a story about an incredibly resilient Iraqi who makes heroic efforts just to go to work everyday, because I think that's reflecting a lot what's going on here now. So I say "positive" in quotes. But if you say there hasn't been a lot of positive coverage, that means you're just ignoring hundreds of stories about the hope around three elections last year, and the writing of this [Iraqi] constitution, which was written about as this forward-looking unprecedented constitution for the Middle East.

And you can say whatever you want about how important it was to get to rid of a dictatorial regime, but—and maybe a majority of Iraqis are glad that that dictatorial regime is gone; I think certainly the majority of them—but they will also say to you, "But why did it have to be replaced with this?" And the fact that it was replaced with lawlessness and violence and deprivation convinced them that the Americans came here because of the American interest only and didn't really care very much about Iraqi interests or the Iraqi people. And our coverage has reflected that.

And then the other thing the kind, the third part of this, the reconstruction, and the fact that thousands of projects have been completed, have fixed schools and hospitals and railroad tracks and water systems. But most of that was less, and later, than [what] had been planed or promised. So I don't know how much you can pat on the back for things that ultimately fell short of their goals. And especially now that they're ending the reconstructions. The reconstruction is winding down and most of the money, the vast majority of the money, has been spent or committed. You know, if you hire someone to build a house for you for a million dollars in two years, and five years later, it costs two million dollars and the house is only 20 percent complete, you don't say, "Wow, that's great. That's a great foundation you have on this house you were supposed to finish two years ago."

There were goals that were set by the Americans that were not met. The electricity is still below prewar levels and you can see that in a State Department PDF that comes out every week. You can watch it bump up against the prewar level, nose ahead of it sometimes and dip down below it, and that's in spite of some four billion dollars they've spent on electricity. And that's what Iraqis see, and what we cover is what Iraqis see. We're covering the results, and I think

ultimately, the most important aspect of this is what the Iraqis see and what Iraqis think, because they're going to determine how this goes.

Everyday, consciously and subconsciously, Iraqis are making a calculation about whether they think there's a future here in this new government, in this new nation, or whether they're smarter to place their bet with the traditional networks in their tribe, the sects, and their family. And those networks are often good in a short term but often harmful in the long term. And they're the ones making this decision, and they're the ones to listen to whether things are going well or not.

ALISSA RUBIN | *LOS ANGELES TIMES*
There's this constant balancing act between being credulous and being cynical, and you don't want to be either one. You want to have sort of the appropriate level of skepticism. Lead the reader helpfully through the maze. Create a narrative that they can find compelling. All in roughly a thousand words. Day in, day out, you don't always do it right.

We tend not to be analytic. We tell a story and we don't step back and ask ourselves, "Okay, well if this is true, then what does it mean for the big picture?" We tend to be very good at telling the story we see before us. Very accurate, often. But then, what does that mean for the likelihood of success of what the Americans were trying to do in Iraq? I think we didn't step back and think hard enough about that soon enough. And it's not an individual failure. It's almost a cultural aspect of American reporting that is in some ways a strength and in some ways a weakness. We have this idea that we're supposed to be objective. So it's on one hand, on the other hand. These people say this, these people say that. But if that's the only way you report it, sometimes you don't serve the reader because you haven't helped guide them about which one might actually be true.

PATRICK GRAHAM | FREELANCE WRITER
There are so many factors that made for a kind of disconnect. I think that's what happened, because Americans should have been aware of how bad Iraq was getting, much, much earlier on, and how badly it was being run by the army and by the Coalition Provisional Authority—both of them did a really poor job, and I don't know if people realize how bad they were at what they were doing till much later, and presumably, that's what journalism is supposed to do as an early warning system, and I think that journalists ended up, a lot of the time, reporting that kind of bad news after the army and the intelligence people leaked it to journalists in Washington.

FARNAZ FASSIHI |
THE WALL STREET JOURNAL
When I wrote my first-person departure piece [about trying to live and work in Baghdad in February 2006], I got thirty-six pages of e-mail. The response was

overwhelming. And I couldn't believe that people would say, "We had no idea."

It still gets to me that people say, "It's that bad in Iraq? We had no idea." And I'm like, "What do you mean, you had no idea? How can you think that? By your own admission you're a *Journal* subscriber for thirty years. Have you been reading my stories? What do you mean?" I think it just doesn't grab them the same way. For three years we've been writing this. I don't know why people respond to first-person pieces with, "Is it really that bad?"

X

THE CONTINUING STORY

RICHARD ENGEL | NBC NEWS

I've been in Iraq for a while. I've been there longer than any of the military guys, and they rotate through, and they're always the same: at first, you know, they come in with a message, and they treat you badly. I've gone through so many divisions—it drives me crazy. Every time, they come in and they treat me like a stranger. Let's say, I've spent a year with the Third Infantry Division, and I know all the generals, I know all the PAOs, the public affairs officers, and I know all the captains on the frontline units. I know them, they know me, we trust each other to a degree. When soldiers are killed, a lot of times I know the units that they're in. I don't report that because they ask you not to; they want the families to be informed officially,

not to have someone watch the Nightly News with Brian Williams and find their son is dead. I agree with that and respect that. After a while you build up trust, and you can have a real relationship and they'll tell you information and you can tell them information and you can build a relationship of trust. Then, they rotate out, and a new division comes in, and they treat you like the enemy, like a stupid enemy, like you don't know anything and everything is great. The guy's been on the ground for two weeks and he's telling me about Baghdad, and I'm like, "Look, you just got here. I had a great relationship with the divisions that just left. Didn't they tell you?" And then, okay, six months later, the guy finally trusts me and then I get six months of real, working

At Camp Mercury, U.S. paratroopers
in the 1-504th regiment of the Eighty-
second Airborne Division (the "Red
Devils") pray before launching an
overnight raid in Fallujah. November
25, 2003. Chris Hondros/Getty Images

relationship with him, and then he's gone, and I have to start the relationship again. So that happens a lot with the military. You work up a relationship and they go [laughs].

PAUL HOLMES | REUTERS

I have young journalists who come to me and say, "I want to go to Iraq." And my response to them is, "I will help you to build the sort of experience that would qualify you to go to Iraq, but you can't go to Iraq. I'm sorry." And most of them, in fact, all of them, have accepted it. I don't think anybody should have to go to Iraq unless they have experience in a previous conflict, because I don't think it's fair to them, I don't think it's fair to their colleagues, and I don't think it's particularly good for the story. So we look at their experience, we look at their maturity. In a place like Iraq, they live and work with their colleagues in a compound where they can't go out for most of the day and all of the night, and that requires a very special sort of person; you can't have prima donnas in that environment, you can't have loudmouths in that environment. I've worked in that sort of environment with loudmouths, and it's unbearable.

CHRIS HONDROS | GETTY IMAGES

I think a lot of journalists want every war to be like the Israeli-Palestinian conflict: a place where you can stay in a nice hotel, get up in the morning, drive in your car, see a battle, cover it, see all these dramatic things, and then drive back just in time to send your pictures and have a nice dinner at the American Colony [Hotel], and smoke and drink wine, and tell war stories, and what happened that day, and booze it up into the night, and do everything all over again the next day. That's nice. I've covered stuff there, too, but the world isn't conformed to how journalists should cover—the world is as it is and we as journalists go and do it. Sometimes things are easy and sometimes things are incredibly hard.

VIVIENNE WALT | FREELANCE WRITER

I was just recently in the Niger Delta, and I was in a small, little village where we had no telephone contact whatsoever and where the locals were really pretty hostile and nobody knew where we were. And it occurred to me there if we were to be kidnapped—and there's a lot of westerners kidnapped in the Niger Delta—but if we were to be kidnapped, there was really like no one to appeal to, and nobody who would come and really search for us very easily. Nobody knew where we were. We could disappear off the face of the earth.

I think that Iraq is certainly very, very dangerous. I think in some ways its uniqueness is a little bit exaggerated by those who cover Iraq. There have been many, many conflicts that have been just as dangerous recently: Chechnya, for example—an extremely dangerous place— and I do also think that there are parts of Iraq which are kind of dicey but completely manageable. For example, I was just in

Kurdistan; Kurdistan is not totally safe, but it is an important part of Iraq and you can more or less operate there pretty well and do some important Iraqi stories. So I feel like, yes, Baghdad is very hard to move around in these days, but it's not the worst in the world, and it's not the only place in the world that's that dangerous.

DAN MURPHY |

THE CHRISTIAN SCIENCE MONITOR

I had gone and watched a movie with a buddy in Mansur one night, fall or early winter of 2004, and we wanted to go over the bridge. The bridge that you go over to go toward the airport, and there was an American vehicle checkpoint set up basically blocking the way you wanted to go on the bridge. It would have meant a twenty-minute detour for us. There were three or four cars that would pull up and they would turn around; it was late at night.

So we stopped and rolled down the window and a private walks over and I said, "I'm an American reporter, can you let me through, 'cause this is going to take another twenty minutes and it's dark and a little dangerous and we're just going over there." The guy says, "Shut the fuck up." I say, "Look man, I don't want to make trouble for you," and while I'm talking to him he's got his flashlight and he's moving it in frenetic circles over both of my eyes. I said, "Look, really man, I'm just trying to get home. Is there any way we can just get through?" And he says, "Now you've done it! I'm pulling you

over and I'm making you wait here while we search your whole car."

So we comply. We got out of the car, stand away from the car as we were told to, open the trunk, etcetera. And this is my friend's driver, an Iraqi driver who I had just met that evening, so I felt pretty bad that I had gotten him into that situation. And the pimply private comes over and he says to me, "Yeah, how do you like that? You see what you get when you fuck with me?" Like two feet from my face. And not to my perfect credit, I basically called him a word that will famously get you thrown out of any baseball game that has ever been played. You can figure that out for yourself. Not a pleasant word. And that was it. He goes and talks to his commanding officer, who comes over and within two minutes has me zip-tied, handcuffed, roughly searched, and interrogated for fifteen minutes. We go through this and I'm calm, as I usually am, and eventually they're like, I guess we can't arrest an American for using language that we don't like. They untie me, and we drove off and go home.

About a week later, we get an e-mail addressed to the *Christian Science Monitor* Baghdad bureau chief, and I was chief at the time, and it's a letter written by the general in Baghdad at the time. The letter goes on to say we've had a lot of complaints about the conduct of our troops in the field and we try to hold ourselves to a high standard and correct problems when they are brought to our attention by the press, but we think you have to be equally responsible and aware of the terrible behavior of your people. For instance, this guy Dan Murphy was stopped and was politely asked to step out of his car and he refused and launched into a profanity-laced, anti-American tirade, and he was so agitated and physically wild that we had to restrain him for his safety and our own. And etcetera, etcetera, etcetera. That was completely fantasy. It was lies. And I have no doubt that the general who wrote this letter believed it; he had attached the incident report written by the soldiers who were involved in this little incident.

Basically, I responded and said I happen to be that guy, and I will tell you exactly what happened, and of course [the report] has no truth because these things have no truth. And he apologized and said, "These things get garbled in transmission, sorry." Now, does this incident matter in the big scheme of things? No. Did the guys on that patrol lie because they thought that maybe arresting Americans for using one naughty word isn't the thing they should be doing? Maybe. Was what he was told by the soldiers in the field, who of course might have an incentive to lie, believed wholeheartedly by this general? Absolutely. Does it lead me to believe—given the source from the podium in the Green Zone and elsewhere over three years now—that these sorts of reports are far from the whole truth? Absolutely. Have there been military investigations that have proven the same? Absolutely.

I think you get the point of the story.

HANNAH ALLAM | KNIGHT RIDDER (McCLATCHY)

We are three years into this thing, and when you go out and you're talking to some soldier on his third tour in Iraq or his second offensive into the same city, they're not happy campers. And they're going to tell you that or it's going to come across other ways. Or you see that the reservoir of goodwill towards Iraqis had melted away because now they've seen enough of their buddies killed or maimed that they consider everyone the enemy and so they're much more hardened. There's not this whole hearts-and-mind focus anymore. It's just, "Let me do my time and get out of here and make it back to my family in one piece and I don't really care about the future of Iraq and the lofty ideals of nation-building." That stuff's gone by now, for the most part. They're still some holdouts but I think they're probably one IED away from being just like the rest of the guys.

GHAITH ABDUL-AHAD | THE GUARDIAN, GETTY IMAGES

So it was a very weird experience [to report alongside the insurgents] but, again, I think I'm so privileged to have that weird experience because those people—call them what you want, call them insurgents, call them terrorists, call them nut cases, call them jihadis, anything. But you have to understand. If you want to know what's happening, it's not enough to brand them terrorists and then go and kill every one of them. It's not enough. So I think that going to the other side, and writing about the other side is a very, very important thing.

And I told you, every time I see an American armored vehicle driving through a street, I think "Oh my God," and I see this gun pointing at the people and I think, "Oh my God, he will kill me now, he will shoot me now." And you are so scared; most of the time I'm scared. And every time I see an armored vehicle, even in 2003, even in April 2003, an armored vehicle, a machine gun is a big huge massive thing, and it's a scary thing. And I'm scared, of course. And every time I see a big American gun, I'm scared.

But when I was inside the American camp, and when I was seeing the same street, I was seeing it through a black-and-white infrared screen, every moving being was black and every still building was white, and then you see these black things getting very close to your armored vehicle and you think, "My God, why are they getting so close, why isn't he killing them? Why isn't he shooting them, defending…." Automatically you are switched, and you become on the other side. So I do understand why the American soldiers look at the insurgents as the enemy, and I do understand why the insurgents look at the U.S. soldiers as the enemy. But for us journalists, we have to do this amazing, very difficult mental exercise to try to keep ourselves in the middle.

BORZOU DARAGAHI | *LOS ANGELES TIMES*
I used to go and hang out here in Baghdad. I used to do kind of fun things once. We used to go to a hair salon and just hang out, or a barbershop. We used to go to restaurants. I still try to go to my favorite little DVD shop, but recently a friend of mine went and it was closed. It's like our world is getting smaller and smaller. The opportunities for interacting with ordinary Iraqi people have gotten fewer and fewer.

Now I'm determined to be able to do this, so we invite people. I recently invited an Iraqi family that I wanted to interview for a story over to the compound for lunch. And we brought the whole family over, sat down to lunch, and had like a two-hour conversation. They weren't afraid. But I offered to go to their house and they said, "No, we don't want you to come to our house." And I said, "Oh wow, are you guys afraid that your neighbors will see me and come and get you later?" And they were like, "No, our neighbors know we interact with foreigners, they know who we are, but we're afraid that you're gonna get killed at one of the rolling checkpoints."

MITCH PROTHERO |
UNITED PRESS INTERNATIONAL
What's been lost is the idea of some of these experienced and talented journalists cruising around Baghdad and looking for stuff—stuff that they want to be hearing right now. And that's what we've lost—any kind of spontaneity in the coverage—because of the security situation. I don't think it's biased or these things are necessarily… but in that area, it's sad. It's a loss for everybody.

FARNAZ FASSIHI |
THE WALL STREET JOURNAL

When I left Iraq for the first time—you know, the tensions in Iraq are so extreme. We were constantly, twenty-four hours a day, on a state of high alert, survival mode. That situation, constantly under tension, you don't really sleep well. You don't know what's going to happen the next moment. In addition to feeling that for yourself, you're also worried about your colleagues. I was very worried about the Iraqi staff. Being responsible for security of the Iraqi staff. And all the bad things, the terrible things you cover. All the horror, all the misery of the Iraqis.

Every time I left Iraq, I would just stay in a hotel in Amman for two days doing nothing. I couldn't immediately jump on a plane home. For me, anxiety would come in the most unusual places. Like suddenly in a commercial flight. Or for a really long time, I couldn't sit by the window in New York. Or anywhere. When I'd walk into a restaurant I'd constantly choose the furthest seat from the window. Because I always associated windows with smashing. I'd seen it happen several times where a car bomb had gone off and smashed the windows. So you avoid sitting by the window.

We talk to each other. Journalists talk to each other about these kind of things. That's one thing….

COLONEL WILLIAM DARLEY |
MILITARY REVIEW

What I try to impress upon [soldiers] is that the inside-the-Beltway media is not the media. It's the inside-the-Beltway media. And they need to understand also that reporters are very much like them. They're idealists, they believe. They're not working for money; they're working for what they regard as a mission, and their mission is to tell the truth, and to get the truth out to the American people so people can make rational decisions about their government and about their society. And that they're talented, for the most part, very talented guys and girls out there.

ANNE GARRELS | **NPR**

I think all of us, we keep wondering when we're going to wake up one morning and say this whole thing is just not doable except embedded. But that hasn't happened; it is just about doable, but one does feel that one is being hunted and it's very stressful, and initially it was us as foreigners who felt we were being hunted. My concern now is that my staff is also being hunted—translators. Translators working for the military have been targeted for a long time, but translators working, or translators—all of them—are very discreet, they don't tell anybody who they're working for. And if you look overall… they have been sort of okay up to now, not that they haven't been killed by American or Iraqi troops, especially cameramen on assignment, but in terms of being hunted down in their houses, there have been some instances, but it has not been widespread. I'm worrying now that it is increasing. The concern is that as the situation unravels more and more in Iraq, it's hard to know who's doing what to whom, but there is a price tag on our heads and on the heads of the people who work for us. After three years, they know that they're valuable to us, we care about them.

DEXTER FILKINS | *THE NEW YORK TIMES*
When you're a target, it's different—it's weird, you know? It's really strange. Any number of times I've been in a car driving down the road, and suddenly a car will come after me, and you don't want to hang around and figure out why they're trying to run you off the road or cut you off. And I've been chased, cut off, guys with guns, the whole thing. It so suddenly kind of turns on you. You will not unwind while you're there in Iraq. You just can't. You're just kind of cranked up for however long you're there. You're just kind of wound up. The last time I was there I did seventeen weeks, so I stayed out for a long time, but—so it's usually a couple of months and you're pretty fried. But it's mostly the isolation. It's just very, very isolated. There's nothing much else to do except work. You're in this house, cooped up a lot of time. You're working all the time. You really have to work a lot because everything moves so slowly that if you do sixteen hours, it's like you moved this gigantic wheel one little click. So the next day you work another sixteen hours and the wheel moves another click. It's all so slow now and truncated that

it just takes more and more labor to get the smallest thing done.

The really horrible security situation in Iraq has made it not just terribly dangerous to report there but terribly, terribly expensive. And the result of that has been that the danger has chased a lot of reporters away. In '03 and '04 there were hundreds of reporters there, you know? And you never really saw them until some muckety-muck would come into town and go to the Green Zone for a press conference, and everybody would crowd in there, and there were four or five hundred reporters there. Now maybe there's like fifty. There's nothing—there's nobody there. The Europeans are all gone. There's a few Brits. There's just basically the big American papers and the TV networks, but the TV networks can hardly get out because they're carrying all this incredibly expensive equipment. Part of that is the danger and part of that is the unbelievable expense. When I just think of the money that the *New York Times* has paid, has shelled out and continues to shell out to allow us to report there, it's just mind-boggling, you know, millions of dollars. We have two houses. We have blast walls. We have, I don't know, thirty or forty armed guards round the clock. We have three armored cars, which together probably cost a million dollars. We have two generators large enough to power two houses that can run around the clock, which usually do run around the clock and which drink an enormous

Iraqi Shiite women hold empty bullet casings in the al-Sheala district of Baghdad after a raid on suspected insurgents by Iraqi and U.S. troops. August 1, 2006. Reuters/Thaier Al-Sudani/Landov

amount of gasoline every day. We have two satellite systems—a regular one and then a back-up whenever that one fails so that we can be in constant communication with the outside world; we have—we run up these unbelievable satellite phone bills and cellular phone bills.

TOM LASSETER | KNIGHT RIDDER (McCLATCHY)

Most of western Iraq—you just can't function out there as a western reporter. The country has gotten smaller and smaller. I miss Iraq, I do. I live in Baghdad, but I miss the country.

FARNAZ FASSIHI | *THE WALL STREET JOURNAL*

I can't imagine going to Iraq for the first time now and writing it. Truly you do not know the country. You would be writing blindly, with no tangible sense of the place or the people. So I think that as we've sort of gotten tired and cycled out, it's going to be interesting to see how that's going to play out.

CHRISTOPHER ALLBRITTON | FREELANCE WRITER

I hope I contributed to the world's understanding of what's happening in Iraq. I would like to avoid going back to Iraq. I'm not personally interested in the story anymore. Burned out. With too few breaks. Most of the world is waiting for this train wreck to run its course. Anyone can see it's going from bad to worse to truly terrible.

ANNE GARRELS | NPR

So you really do see a huge amount by being on the ground, and you don't always realize how much you're seeing at the time until you then go and sit with another unit and you go, "Wait a minute—they're doing…." So that's why I keep going back, because the more you know, the more you know. When I think about how little I knew to start with, it seems a shame to give up now when I actually know something and know better questions to ask and have seen three and a half years of this. On the other hand, you have to ask yourself, "Are you getting a little nutty?"

LARRY KAPLOW | COX NEWSPAPERS

It takes hundreds and hundreds of stories to get a point across, to get a reality across, to a country the size of the United States. And if reporters start dwindling in numbers here, it's going to be harder and harder to get across whatever is happening here, whether it's good or bad.

LIZ SLY | *CHICAGO TRIBUNE*

There is a sort of cumulative [effect] to being there. It just hasn't reached the point yet that I just want to stop finding out what is going on. The more time you spend there, the more you learn about the place, and the more you learn about the place, the harder it is to let go of the story because you become more entrenched in it, you become more entwined in it. It's kind of a matter of seeing where the movie ends up.

I think you are looking at a situation where the foreign press corps, maybe a group of about twenty or thirty people who go to Iraq regularly, probably know more about Iraq than anyone else. More than the people at the embassy who are stuck inside the Green Zone and only get a particularly slanted point of view. More than the military behind their barbed wire.

Occasionally my desk will ask me, "Can we get an expert to explain this to us?" Or, "Is there a report on how many deaths there have been, and that kind of thing?" You haven't got experts who know about Iraq. You have experts who are very well informed about Iraq. But the details of what is going on on the ground, the day-to-day bits of things, really, the journalists are the only ones who know that.

CAROLINE HAWLEY | BBC

My big worry is that the audience sometimes doesn't know what they are missing and that we as journalists didn't always know what we were missing, because we were unable to function as we would anywhere else in the world. You are unable to just go and chat with people in coffee shops. You're unable to just drive up to a town an hour north of Baghdad, a mixed Shiite and Sunni town, and chat to people about sectarian division. You are unable to do all the things that you felt you should have been doing. And my worry always was that we didn't know how much we were missing.

ANNE BARNARD | *THE BOSTON GLOBE*

The most personal thing I have to say about this probably is that when I first came into Iraq, it was really a feeling that a Band Aid had been ripped off the skin of Iraq—that everything was raw, everything was new. It might be a little painful or disorienting, but people were starting to talk, and people were spilling out these stories. People had many hopes and many fears, and it was the most dynamic experience I've ever experienced as a reporter, or personally. There's a lot of sadness when I look back on that, when I look back on what might have been. And not to give the wrong impression—readers should know that Iraqis still are, in fact, going to work every day and going to the market. But the overarching fear and uncertainty I'm sure they didn't know would last has lasted three years and counting.

But Iraq had suddenly broken open and all these things—both therapeutic and really ugly—were bursting out of people, and literally these bodies were bursting out of the ground. And people were digging up, on their hands and knees, digging up the ribs and the femurs of their relatives that had been buried by Saddam. They were finding them in these graves. At the time you had this idea that it was going to be like the end of the Soviet Union, and people were going to start reexamining their own personal choices in having condoned or supported or tolerated that regime, and that that would be a healthy process for the country.

But instead, the ugliness of what came

out from things that were buried, physically and metaphorically, was just too much. There was so much anger that had to come out. And when you combine that with the failures of the American occupation to provide a safe environment for those things to be worked out, you got the situation that we have today.

GHAITH ABDUL-AHAD | *THE GUARDIAN,* GETTY IMAGES

The war itself was a significant event, seeing Saddam's statue fall was a significant event, walking into Saddam's palace was such a significant event. Okay, here's the thing—it's not the elections, not Saddam's palace, not Saddam's statue falling, not the insurgency, not being attacked on Haifa Street. It's just every time I drive in front of one of the official buildings that was, for example, the presidential palace or the headquarters of the [Iraqi] Army or the Republican Guard, and seeing the U.S soldiers, the Humvees, in front of that building. I start trying to half close my eyes and think that I was there in Baghdad in 2003, and if someone came and told me, "Look, Ghaith, in a year's time there will be U.S. soldiers instead of those militia guarding that building," I would say, "Come on, is that science fiction or something?"

That is what is the most significant thing, every time I try to realize this, it's still very difficult to comprehend. Saddam was such a huge thing. When I was growing up as a child, the figures of God and Saddam were almost the same thing. I grew up in a Catholic school and there was this figure of God, this big mighty huge man. And then there was this big mighty huge man with a big moustache on TV. And then both of them, when I was like, eight, nine, ten, both of them became one single figure for me. So growing under Saddam for twenty-eight years, and then seeing Saddam removed, and seeing Saddam replaced, and then seeing the militia, the Iraqi Army occupation of Baghdad being replaced by another form of military occupation, that is the hard thing for me, and that is what I think most of the Iraqis feel.

JOHN LEE ANDERSON | *THE NEW YORKER*

It [war coverage] is never going to be perfect and it can't be because we're talking about war, and war is like a virus—once you let it out of the box, it goes anywhere, and everybody always has to do catch-up in a war, there's no perfect way to cover it. There's no safe way to cover war, there's no proper way. In some ways it's a very abnormal thing to be doing, just as war is, although it seems a historically inherent demand, it's an abnormal activity—the act of mass, legalized, politically legalized slaughter, and with us there somehow witnessing it and recording it, and trying to make sense out of it. So having said all of that, it's bound to have—our process is bound to be rife with contradictions and problems, and to be continuously a learning process.

ALI FADHIL | TRANSLATOR, REPORTER

Of course I'm frightened. Nobody is not

frightened in Iraq—even if you're not a journalist.

CHRIS HONDROS | GETTY IMAGES

There was a particular incident that happened on January 18, 2005, up in Tal Afar in the north of Iraq. I got out there on Saturday, and they wanted me to go out [on an embed] on this mission they had going out on Sunday. The next day, we went on a routine patrol. I got with one unit that seemed to be pretty good: the Apache Company. They were pretty press-friendly, these guys, and we went on a walking patrol in downtown Tal Afar, just in the middle of the afternoon, handing out flyers supporting the upcoming election and all that. And sure enough, in the middle of the afternoon we got into a firefight. They got ambushed a little bit—a few shots were fired, and before they knew it they were surrounded, and they were firing out, they were firing in— dramatic, hour-long gun-battle in downtown Tal Afar. And because none of their guys were injured, and they basically came back, they were all exhilarated, and I had all these dramatic pictures, and they liked them. Then Monday I just hung around the base. The mortar guys, the guys who fire the long-range mortars, they were just firing a few mortars—I took some pictures of that, nothing special.

And then finally on Tuesday, the same guys—the Apache guys who were in the firefight—were going out on a late afternoon patrol. So I said, "All right, I'll go on that." But they got delayed. So finally at six we went out, and it was the same kind of thing, a little smaller, like a small group of twenty men or so, patrolling. And it was also dark by this point. So they're out on the streets, and it's after the curfew, which is about six o'clock. And as we were patrolling on a darkened boulevard, in the distance, a car, maybe a hundred yards down at least, turned onto the boulevard and started coming toward us. And I already had a bad feeling, you know? Because these are camouflaged soldiers; they don't patrol regularly, and they don't call much attention to themselves, because if they have lights and sirens and things like that they'd be seen or easily attacked. So here's a bunch of testy men with guns running around and a car coming towards them, and they don't let cars come toward them.

I had a feeling the situation was going to end up badly. So I moved over to the side, because I feared at least some warning shots would be fired. The car kept coming. It was dark. Sure enough, somebody fired some warning shots, the car kept coming. And then they fired into the car. And it limped into the intersection, clearly no longer under its own power, just on momentum, and gently came to rest on a curb. I was kind of paralyzed, and then slowly walked to the car and, sure enough, I hear children's voices inside the car, and I knew it was a family. The doors opened; the back doors opened, and kids just tumble out of the car, one after one after one—six in all. One was shot to the abdomen, though we didn't realize he was shot at the time, though he was bleeding profusely and as soon as he dropped, there was blood in the street. The soldiers realized it was a civilian car. They ran and grabbed all the kids and ran them to the sidewalk. In the front seat, what ended up being the parents were killed, riddled with bullets, instantly dead. The children in the back were, incredibly enough, okay, except for the one kid who was winged in the abdomen.

I photographed the car coming in, and even the tail end of it getting shot up and it resting on the curb, the children coming out, the soldiers carrying them over to the side, treating them, looking them over, trying to figure out who was shot, who was not. And the father—the mother's body was collapsed, you could hardly see her, but the father was still sitting up on the seat, riddled with bullets, his skull had almost collapsed because it had been shot so many times.

What happened was—and we found out from the boy who was shot, he ended up being flown to Boston for treatment—they were out visiting with family or something and they knew that their curfew was in the evening, so they were trying to get home. It was a little bit after the curfew, but time is never a precise thing to Iraqis—it's not like this German, iron-clad, six-o-one curfew. It's more like, all right, you're not supposed to be driving around at night. Generally speaking, you could be out on the roads after six o'clock and nothing would happen to you. They were just trying to hustle and get home, and they're driving along, and all of a sudden they hear shots. They don't see—it's dark—they don't see camouflaged

soldiers in the dark in front of them. They just hear shots. Now, when you're in a car driving around Iraq and you hear shots, your first instinct is to speed up, because either someone's shooting at you for some reason or somebody's about to get into a battle nearby. Either way, you don't want to be around there; you want to get out of there. And then, the headlight range—by the time they actually get into the region of your headlights, forget it, that's way too close, they're already engaging you by that point, shooting you up by that point. So that's why they didn't stop.

So I photographed this thing, and again, the military didn't try to obstruct me or stop me from photographing—and they could have—and it's kind of remarkable that they didn't; it's kind of a human reaction and so on. But they didn't, and that has happened before: sketchy things have happened on embeds. Almost every soldier in Iraq has been involved in some sort of incident like that or another, I would say. Their attitude about it was grim, but it wasn't the end of their world. It was, "Well, kind of wished they'd stopped. We fired warning shots. Damn, I don't know why the hell they didn't stop. What're you doing later, you want to play Nintendo? Okay." Just a day's work for them. That stuff happens in Iraq a lot. That's why it's such a damn mess, because almost everybody's had something like that happen to them at the hands of U.S. soldiers. They hate them.

But I realize, as much as that happens in Iraq, it almost never gets photographed, and so I did realize I was onto an important set of pictures. I was also technically worried if I had anything at all because it was completely pitch dark, almost to the limits of what can be photographed, and I had the camera set in a way that lets in the maximum amount of light but often blurs photos, so I was worried that it would be a bunch of mush. So I played along with their casual attitude, because I didn't want them to realize what I suspected: that this would be an important set of pictures that would go out a lot. I wasn't saying, "What's your name? What's his name? What happened here?" I was just trying to photograph, and I was just trying to stay in the background—click-click quietly, didn't say anything, didn't offer up any opinion or anything. And then it's, "We're going now." "All right, ready to go?" "Okay."

They radioed ahead to the base about what had happened, and I met up with the major there on the base, an officer who ran it, and who probably knew a little better than these guys that what had happened out there could get out, that a journalist was along. So he calls me to his office as soon as I get back, and he says, "Pretty unfortunate what happened out there, Chris. We're going to investigate, see what happened. We'd appreciate it if you held off on sending those photos for a couple of days, because we're going to investigate, try to see if we can get to the bottom of what happened out there." I want to get these photos out. Whether we send them on the news wire or not, that can be negotiated, but I need to get these back to New York before something happens. I

mean, they have the capability to jam all communications from base, including my personal sat phone. They don't want me to send these photos out. Their base, 100 percent their property; they're the army, they have no reason whatsoever not to confiscate my sat phone or jam communications to prevent me from sending the pictures. So I said, "Well, I have to talk to my boss, but yeah, I think we want to work with you there, Major. So I think we can probably do something like that, let me check but I think we'll be okay." And then I stepped out of the major's office, ran back to my trailer, and flipped open my sat [satellite] phone, got all the pictures and looked at them, and whoa, I couldn't believe how much information was there. The pictures did come out. And I said, "Okay, send, send! Tone them up, tone them up, quickly, quickly, send, send, send!"

And I put on the captions: "Don't send these out until you hear from me, until you hear from my boss"—Pancho Bernasconi is my boss. So I sent twenty pictures, and I got my Thuraya phone. I talked to Bernasconi and I said you better talk to this guy about what to do, and he said, "I'll talk to him." So I walked back over to the major's office, but the major had gone to bed. And then there was a captain who I'd also talked to earlier, still up, and I said, "I have my boss on the phone, can you guys talk about …" and the captain, young sport, he said, "Yeah, okay, sure." So they talked, and I heard them talking, and I heard his side. He said, "Well, we'd like to hold onto these photos. We're asking you not to send them out for a few days so we can investigate . . . Uh-huh, uh-huh, uh-huh. Yeah, well, we wanted a little bit of time for us to get the investigation, uh-huh." And I think what my boss was saying was, "Well, we're a wire service, by the time we put them on our wire—but they won't actually be in papers till a day or two, [or] maybe not—people use them or not, it just depends." I heard that back and forth, and the captain said, "All right, well, I think we've come to an agreement" or something, and gave the phone back to me. So I went to bed.

Six a.m. next morning [makes knocking sounds]: "The major wants to see you right away!" Oh boy, here we go. The major's up bright and early. The major had already received an e-mail from Baghdad, the army office in Baghdad, because the photos were distributed right away by my office and immediately went out all over the world right away. Meanwhile, Baghdad Central Command had not been informed. If there's something controversial, they're supposed to report that to Baghdad and say, "Hey, by the way, there's going to be some bad press coming out of here because we had a friendly-fire incident." Then the Baghdad press office is always able to kind of prepare for it. They had no warning whatsoever. They just looked on the Web sites in the morning and they see these series of horrible pictures of U.S. soldiers shooting up an Iraqi family.

So the major comes up to me. "What happened, Chris? I thought we had an agreement. I thought you said you were going to hold onto those photos." I said,

"Well, major, I came back and you were in bed. I talked to the captain." And the captain was right there and [the major] said, "What! Captain? Did he come back here last night?" and [the captain] said, "Well, yes, sir, but I talked to his boss and he…" and [the major] said, "Chris, excuse me for a second." And the poor captain's watching his career evaporate. The captain was saying, "Well, I thought—my impression was that the boss in New York said they were going to hold them."

And you know, it was a confusing thing.

Afterword

FIVE REPORTERS REFLECT ON THE WAR

On November 3, 2006, in conjunction with the publication of its November/December 2006 issue, the Columbia Journalism Review *hosted a panel discussion about coverage of the war in Iraq. The panelists were Deborah Amos, a foreign correspondent who has covered the war for* NPR *and is also the author of* Lines in the Sand: Desert Storm and the Remaking of the Arab World *(1992); Rajiv Chandrasekaran of* The Washington Post, *and the author of* Imperial Life in the Emerald City: Inside Iraq's Green Zone *(2006); Ali Fadhil, an Iraqi doctor turned translator, stringer, and reporter for western journalists; Patrick Graham, a Canadian freelancer; and Chris Hondros, a prize-winning photojournalist. The panel was moderated by Evan Cornog, the publisher of* CJR. *What follows is an edited version of their conversation.*

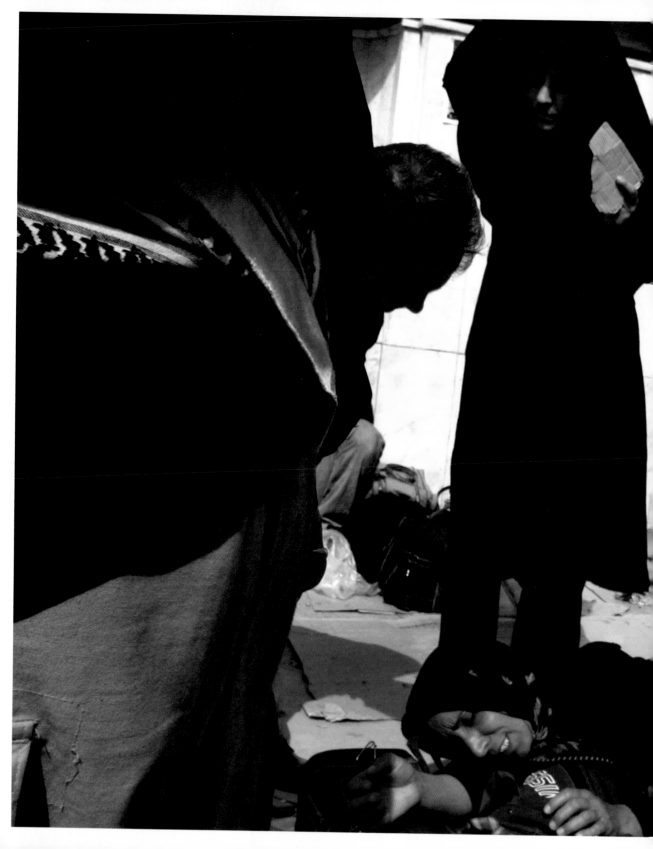

Iraqi Shiites, who had traveled to Karbala to celebrate Ashura for the first time in thirty-five years, mourn the loss of relatives after bombings there killed at least eighty-five Shiites. March 2, 2004. Andrea Bruce/ *The Washington Post*

CJR: Ali. You had been in Iraq, you knew the country, you were working there as a doctor. It wasn't, as I recall, until January 2004 that you essentially developed a second career as a journalist, as a translator, and eventually reporting and all of that. I'm interested to know, for you, how did that transition take place?

FADHIL: Well, I started in late 2003. First job I got was as a translator with the *Financial Times.* James Harding and I worked on a story around Iraq: How people think about Saddam Hussein, how people think about the occupation, if people want the Americans to stay or leave.

We were in Karbala when Saddam was captured. The moment he was captured there was a big celebration in Karbala. People were celebrating. People were shooting in the air. Everyone was saying, "They captured Saddam, they captured Saddam."

That was the moment for me of change. I was looking to the people in a different angle. Right now I am with western journalists, with the media, and I see my own people in a different way. They're more open, they tell you more. Actually I'm saying this because I compare it to my job as a physician. I'm sitting in an emergency room talking to people. People come complaining, but not just about their pain and sickness, they also talk about their lives.

Actually, they talk more about their problems more than anything else in the emergency room. I was interested in seeing my country in a different angle, especially right now, after the occupation. To clarify this point, I was in Yemen before the invasion and when the war happened I was really disappointed. I didn't want the war to happen because I thought there would be chaos in Iraq just like 1991, and people will get killed, people will kill each other.

I arrived in Iraq and worked in Baghdad Medical City, which is the largest medical complex in Iraq, and I thought that Iraq was starting a new age. It's going to be wonderful, it's going to be the best country in the world—just like anywhere else. Then in the hospital, things really turned out not as I had imagined. My idea to go back from Yemen—my wife didn't like it. My daughter was only a month and a half. When we arrived we were thinking about what kind of future she will have in Iraq and immediately I was disappointed after two months from arriving in Iraq in the post war.

Later on, I was ready to work on anything else. I was ready to do anything else. I was disappointed. And then I was approached to work as a translator and I did. It was a side job for me. It was something I wouldn't pursue. I wouldn't think about the media. As I said, I was interested from the first job, from the first assignment when I started seeing my people from a different angle. I understood my country in a very, very different way.

And then things happened. I worked with Patrick Graham in Fallujah, I worked with NPR. I worked with different people. The assignment moved up from being a translator into a reporter. I could go outside, do stories, bring it back to reporters and discuss it. And that was it, that was how I started. I shifted from medicine to journalism. I like it. I'm going through it for the coming years. I might go back to medicine one day but I don't know when.

If I would do something different from what reporters want, if I am detached from what they want? I don't think so. That never happened to me. Because when we have an assignment to do something we will sit before that and we will say, "Okay, here is the spin today, this is what we want, what do you think about it?" "That's fine. We can do this, we can't do this." We already discussed it in the office before we go out and do the stories, so I don't think they were detached. There were a few occasions when there were problems between us as translators and the reporters. Sometimes they don't understand the situation. They would ask about things that are far away from the story around that area particularly. But I think as a translator you are obligated to do what they want from you. And I think it was for me very interesting until the end of 2004 when I started a new career as a filmmaker.

GRAHAM: I just want to say, I wish I could become a doctor and then say I'll be a journalist in a few years.

FADHIL: You can be my translator in Canada.

GRAHAM: Oh good, because when Ali was my translator he dressed me up as his brother with a brain aneurism, made me a fake ID, and snuck me into Fallujah and nearly got us killed, so I'm not sure I can do that in Canada but I'll try.

I think that there are so many different perspectives—Iraq is now fragmenting. I think the fragments were there and journalists came across them in different ways. People who spent time in Kurdistan tend to see things like Peter Galbraith sees them, from a Kurdish point of view, and people who spent time with the Shia tend to see things from a more Shia point of view.

I was there during the war, and the day that they pulled down the statue I was standing back on Firdos Square and there were far fewer people than it appeared on television. I was standing beside this guy that I was trying to do a story on. I was clinging to him and asking him what he thought, and he said, "Well, I think we are taking one small step forward."

But the people who were out of the range of cameras were very, very ambivalent and it was captured in that "we're taking one small step forward" sense. Those of us who were there during the war were astounded by these riverboat-gambler journalists who came in with the troops—really gung-ho—and suddenly everything that we had been unable to cover was suddenly there for anybody. It was very jarring.

And it is true, the Iraqis were very open in a way they hadn't been before, and a lot of the friendships I made in Iraq were in those first few weeks, first few months. Certainly the people in Fallujah were very open. I had made friends with some Iraqis during the war. I think they saw the way things were turning and they wanted to become friends with a westerner because they thought it would offer some protection and they were from Fallujah. They actually wanted me to go and stay there during the war because it would be safer than Baghdad. I did go up there for a day. I kind of snuck out of town and I went to a big meeting of all the local dignitaries, and I learned later that they were deciding whether or not they were going to fight for Saddam against the Americans and they decided not to. There was an enormous amount of ambivalence. Especially in the Sunni world. Whatever they felt about Saddam, he was a failure. He screwed them. Even if he was their leader. Whatever kind of loyalties they had.

There was a kind of chance of sitting around talking to those people, certainly after Saddam fell, when they were just curious about the outside world, and you were it. And they took you into their house and it was really lovely. I used to go to Fallujah on holiday in the spring of 2003. Just to get out of Baghdad, to get away from the looting, and then I came back in the summer because I was hired to do a story for the *Times Magazine* about who is attacking the Americans. So I just went out there. And by then they knew me as both a non-American—because I'm Canadian—and a journalist. And so I said, "Can I talk to somebody?" And they brought in these people who were insurgents.

It wasn't real journalism. I actually spent a year with insurgents not because I was interested in them but because I couldn't get published on them. Every time I got a story done it would be killed by the magazine. It went through three different magazines because there was no way of fact checking anything. That was one of the strange things about Iraq: the truth and facts are not that closely related. And I think one of the great problems with American journalism in Iraq was that if you were going to criticize the U.S. Army or take on the enormous amount of spin—that wasn't just coming out of the army it was coming out of other journalists too—you had to have your facts straight, and facts in Iraq were fairly elusive. It was very hard to prove you were even with insurgents.

What developed there was…I kind of liked these people. The insurgents that I met, some I didn't like, some I did like. The Iraqis in Fallujah, I liked them, and I liked hanging out with them. I spent the fall of 2003 when it was actually really—I kind of disagree, it was really violent in the fall of 2003, even by September. By November it was extremely violent. If you went out there, there were attacks all the time. The locals called the highway between Ramadi and Fallujah the "Highway of Death."

There were a lot of people being killed. The Eighty-second Airborne was there. And the Eighty-second is a World War Two frontline outfit. They get someone to shoot at them and they call in an air strike on a farm. And a lot of people were killed. A lot of kids were killed. A lot of civilians. You didn't know anybody out there who didn't know somebody who was killed. And often a bomb would go off, and then this whole idea that the U.S. Army has this force protection. They would sort of shoot their .50 calibers pretty wildly and kill a lot of people. Well, Chris has the most dramatic pictures of that I've ever seen.

The checkpoint deaths that you captured were just so constant out there from August on really, and that just wasn't reported. You just did not read about how violent Fallujah was and Ramadi and right up to Haditha and all the way up. And I don't know why.

It had to deal with the way the U.S. press, in general, demonized the Sunnis. When weapons of mass destruction weren't found, another reason for going into Iraq was elevated. And that was the liberation of Iraq, which was genuine. I mean getting rid of Saddam was a very good thing. Well, then you had to get rid of the Baathists and the Baathists went from the fifty-two cards to a large group of people who essentially were the Sunnis.

There was a very strong sense in the American press of this sort of morality play. The Sunnis are bad and the Shia are good and the Kurds are good. And so people would go to Fallujah and Ramadi but they would stay, at most, a night. Mostly they would just drive out for the day. I think it's not really honest to say that in Iraq you can spend an hour with a person. They'll talk but they're just not really going to tell you

anything that you don't want to know or that they don't think you should know. It's a fabulously manipulative society. It has to be. It's a survival instinct. Under Saddam you didn't survive if you weren't incredibly manipulative.

And journalists were manipulated unbelievably by translators, mostly by drivers. A very famous columnist was robbed by his own driver. The driver mafias ran Iraq, ran the journalists' bureaus basically. There was a huge amount of manipulation, which I don't think a lot of journalists even noticed.

CJR: Let me turn to Chris.

HONDROS: I've been to Iraq—I was there during the initial invasion [April 2003], that was my first time in Iraq, and I've been back basically every six months ever since.

Actually, I tried going in unilaterally in an unarmored SUV for the first week or so of the war and that didn't work out. So I went back to Kuwait with my tail between my legs and got embedded and then went back in. Ended up in Baghdad eventually, stayed about a month or so, and went back and then came back in November of 2003, and then the summer of 2004, and December of 2004, and so on.

And for me, I've had an interesting relationship with Iraq because I wasn't there—like a lot of journalists were there a long time in 2003 because it was safe, it was this enormous story. People were there the whole first summer and fall, people spent a year at a time there.

For me, I've always treated Iraq pretty much like any other story. Obviously, it hasn't exactly been like every other story, but I cover things around the world and in a lot of ways Iraq is somewhat of a typical—the issues that we are talking about here are very often the case all over the world. All over the civil wars of Africa or other places around the world.

In Angola, I was there in 1999, you couldn't go anywhere in the countryside. For instance, the government held the cities and the UNITA rebels held the countryside. If you wanted to go from one city to another you had to fly on a UN flight. With the spiral landings just like in Baghdad. It would have been suicide to drive from one city to another—the idea of no-go areas. But now you can go all over the countryside in Angola. All these things that are happening in Iraq, the populace manipulating…Every driver I've ever had in Africa has tried to rip me off like you wouldn't believe.

Iraq is just a massive version of your typical overseas assignment. It's just much more money, much more people, much more interest. From my perspective I see it that way. And you know I still continue to see it that way. I still go back every six months. I am going back soon. To me it remains an important thing that has to be covered.

CJR: And in terms of the pictures you wanted to take…

HONDROS: Again, also an issue around the world. So often you're in some horrible situation in a refugee camp or something somewhere and you think, "Oh, what a horrible situation, surely this will move people to some sort of action on this," and nothing happens. And then sometimes you take a picture that seems quite routine to you, an unfortunate routine—an example of inequity or suffering—that for some reason your mailbox, your e-mail box fills up and everybody wants to help.

In Iraq there were countless examples of both things. In fact, by the time I photographed the checkpoint shooting incident there, I think I had been so jaded a bit by that process that I was wondering if anybody would even notice. I think I sent those pictures off, I felt that they were important, but I wondered if they would cause anybody to sit up and take notice. Thank goodness at least in that case they did.

CJR: When the Coalition Provisional Authority was set up, one of the things they put a tremendous amount of energy into is briefings for the press. One of the people who was interviewed by CJR, Alissa Rubin of the *Los Angeles Times*, talked about the shortcomings of these briefings but said, "It's important to know what the government's narrative is."

CHANDRASEKARAN: I think the briefings were by and large usually useless. If they were the five o'clock follies in Vietnam, I think they were also around five o'clock in Baghdad and a sort of repeat of the same performance.

Look, there is a tendency to be very critical of reporters for not asking tough enough questions at briefings. People love to bash the White House press corps, saying, "Why aren't you tougher in asking questions of the president?" Quite frankly, you can ask all the tough questions you want, they're not going to give it up. They're going to stay on message. It's not like you're going to get this great confession from behind the podium.

Dan Senor was picked because of his political loyalty and his ability to set up a mini–White House press operation for the Coalition Provisional Authority. And his military counterpart, Brigadier General Mark Kimmitt, was also very seasoned political figure in some ways. They coordinated their message very carefully with Washington, they prepared assiduously for their briefings, they had talking points, and they weren't going to give it up.

And if [Dan Senor] was ever candid, it was never for publication. In April of 2004, as Fallujah was being racked by violence—there was the marine offensive there and the Moqtada al-Sadr rebellion, the first one, so the country was essentially awash in both Sunni and Shiite violence—a group of reporters were in the palace and Senor was talking to them and he was being pressed and pressed about what was going on. At that point CPA staffers couldn't get out of the Green Zone. Reconstruction projects had ground to a halt. It seemed like the vast American, neo-conservative experiment to transform Iraq into that peaceful secular democracy, that shining city on a hill, was really falling apart.

And finally Senor said, "Well, off the record, Paris is burning, but on the record, security and stability are returning to Iraq."

AMOS: And it's too bad to beat up on Senor but it's just too delicious because he really was a character, I think, for all of us. And if you did break through the veil there was hell to pay. I remember a day when I kept asking a question in one of those morning huddles that they would have, and he wouldn't look me in the eye and he wouldn't answer any of my questions. And I couldn't figure out what I had done. Then I realized that the day before we had put an interview on the radio where we made his man in Hilla look like a complete idiot. I think the man didn't understand—he was a CPA official. He was in a fight with the most powerful Shia religious leader in the country, Ayatollah Ali al-Sistani, who at the time had said, "We don't need the Americans to pick out who is going to on the city councils."

And this man gave us an interview where he said, "I work very hard to pick the right people to be on the city council. I ask them very specific questions, maybe as long as six hours. And one of the questions I ask them is, 'How did Iraq get into such a pickle?'" And we just let him run on the radio. He sounded like a man so out of touch with reality. We really didn't have to say very much. I'm sure that he thought this was quite a legitimate interview but Dan Senor knew the kind of damage a guy like that could do.

Very soon after that it became harder and harder and harder to roll up to any facility outside of Baghdad and talk to anybody in the CPA.

That now had to be coordinated through Baghdad because you couldn't tell when one of these guys would come off-message, not because they wanted to, but because some of them were so out of touch that if you talked to them in an unguarded moment they weren't as good at this as Dan Senor. So there was some sport in finding people that you could talk to who were outside of Baghdad. But soon we were found out and it was very hard. I don't know if that was your experience, but it certainly was ours. It was very hard to talk to Americans.

CHANDRASEKARAN: And the CPA clearly had a "you're either with us or against us" attitude toward journalists. Journalists who were deferential in briefings, who didn't write stories that they deemed to be anti-coalition, were granted a degree of access. Those who wrote stories that the palace press office perceived as negative were frozen out. Efforts to interview CPA officials, to have other things arranged through that press office—which you needed in many cases to speak to officials, you had to get that permission, you had to get somebody to set it up—their requests would just go to the end of the queue or be thrown out. They were very clear on who they were working with and who they wouldn't. Often times the journalists who would fly in, they would have one shot or two shots before they got on the

black list. Those of us who were there for an extended period of time running a bureau had to toe a very fine line because you didn't want to get entirely shut off. So, you knew how far to push and you didn't want to push too hard.

CJR: Can you talk a little bit—and also Ali—about how these briefings were being seen by an Iraqi audience and how they came across?

GRAHAM: Ali is going to know a lot better than me because he would have heard the translations into Arabic too. One of the first things people bought in Iraq was a satellite dish. There was always this boom in Arabic stations—certainly in Fallujah and Ramadi. Because I knew various families and we would watch the Senor briefings translated into Arabic, I remember one time we were watching it and there was an attempt on the life of a really top general in Fallujah.

CHANDRASEKARAN: Abizaid.

GRAHAM: Yeah, it was [General John] Abizaid [head of U.S. Central Command]. Senor said something like, "There were some criminals who have done something," and these insurgents said something like, "What? We knew he was coming. We were trying to kill him." And they were so angry that they weren't getting credit for this quite courageous operation.

It was the contempt. Whatever you have in Iraq now, you have this Sunni and Shia divide, particularly from the Sunnis you talked to, and the Shias were always angry. (Ali calls himself Sushi so it's kind of a mixture.) The contempt that was directed toward the Sunni minority in those briefings was extraordinary. They really were viewed as not just insurgents but the whole kind of… they saw themselves as not just being pushed out of power, but now they were going to be on the sharp end of the stick and having had the sharp end of the stick pointed the other way, they knew how sharp that was.

Everything in Iraq was run for a domestic American audience, and how it played in Jersey was much more important than what was happening in Iraq. And the Iraqis picked that up very, very quickly. It was not being run for them. And the Sunnis felt that very, very strongly, and I think the Shia weren't too impressed either. Just that contempt for Iraqis.

FADHIL: In terms of how Iraqis would receive these press conferences, press releases. Actually Iraqis know only two Americans. Only two Americans are famous in Iraq. First is Bush, the second is Bremer. That's it. Anyone else means turn the channel.

No one cares about what the others are saying. These press releases come on the Arabic channels or on the national television in Baghdad. It comes like "electricity is improving in Baghdad, now people have twelve hours of electricity." People are like, "What? We have two hours a day." Something like, "Security is good. People are going outside and doing shopping." At the same time people are not. Security is going in the other direction, opposite of what the Americans are saying. People lost confidence in these press releases.

I would like to mention the last briefing in the U.S. Embassy I attended. That was the last day for me in Baghdad, January 21 [2006]. There was this press conference for General McCoy, the Commander of the Corps of Engineers Division in Baghdad and also the American ambassador for the reconstruction office in Baghdad. They were supposed to talk about the reconstruction projects, what they did, what they had accomplished. It was supposed to be on camera. You can record it. People attended. We were about forty or fifty Iraqi and western journalists in that small room in the annex of the U.S. Embassy. They gave us first the press release, there was something written right off the paper. We were quoting and our cameras were running until the moment when it came for the U.S. Ambassador for Reconstruction Daniel Speckhard and General McCoy to come to the podium and talk to us about the actual numbers.

They asked us to actually turn off our cameras and our recorders. And we did. Everyone was pissed off. We were asking why and they said, "This is off-the-record. We'll supply you with press sheets and everything." And there was this moment when General McCoy, he came back to the U.S., was speaking about the electricity projects in Iraq. He announced that they just finished a big project in Haditha in far west Baghdad. "Now Iraqis have twelve hours of electricity everyday." Everyone we know, even westerners because they know how electricity comes on and off—actually at that time in January it was about four hours. It was really bad. Sometimes you don't have electricity for the whole day.

Everyone was angry, "What's happening?" Everyone was shouting—westerners, Iraqis—"How is that?" His answer came out, "Well, this number, that's a summation of ours of working hours for generators around Iraq. It doesn't mean the actual hours of electricity that comes to houses in Baghdad." Then, to elaborate on that, Daniel Speckhart, the U.S. ambassador for reconstruction, said, "Well, I know you are asking a lot about electricity. But look around in Baghdad. Go up to the top of Hamra Hotel. Look at the houses in Baghdad. They are not dark. You can see people have lights in their houses."

One of them said, "But these are generators." He said, "Yeah, they have generators. That's because they have money. They have a good economy." Good economy? Generators? There was a big shortage of generators. Everyone knows that. That's how it was. It was off the camera.

CHANDRASEKARAN: Short story: An Iraqi journalist at one of the Senor-Kimmitt briefings asked, "American helicopters are flying so low over our homes at night. It is scaring the children of Iraq." The answer: "Oh, the children of Iraq shouldn't be worried because that's the sound of freedom."

HONDROS: Quick interesting thing too that I noticed when talking to the soldiers and the troops in general in Iraq. They rotate in and out. No soldier has been in Iraq three and a half years straight. They go in for their six months, year, or whatever it is. It's funny. When young journalists go abroad for the first time—you guys have all seen this too—they get very excited and they put everyone on their e-mail list. They're maybe in Kenya doing freelance journalism and oh, they get so excited.

"Oh I befriended the local baker. He's my friend now. Mr. Baker, yes, he loves me."

Mr. Baker would rip you off in two seconds if you gave him the chance. Maybe not. I don't want to be too cynical. What I'm saying is that young people, journalists, and everybody who travels for the first time, tend to be a bit naïve and tend to overemphasize some of the connections they make with people in the world. And I swear, the U.S. military, all the way up to the high levels, I think, is doing the same thing. Most of those guys never traveled anywhere in the world. I think a lot of the people even on the major and officer level, this is their first time in a foreign country of any significance.

And I saw this over and over again. They were training Iraqis. Major So-and-So would say, "You know, I've really made a relationship with Achmad. He is the commander of his forces. Man to man, we are connecting as men, we talk about our families. There's a real bond here. I can trust him."

And then you'd go meet this Achmad

and he didn't even speak his English. And they're talking to each other. "Yes, yes good, yes, very good very good…"

And this is his idea of I-looked-into-his-eyes, kind of like George Bush: "I looked into his eyes and saw good." And Achmad is running around right now commanding a militia probably. And using guns. They are going to use what they can get.

I swear that is not an insignificant aspect to this, this sort of broad naïveté, don't you think?

CHANDRASEKARAN: More than half of the CPA staff applied for their first passport in order to go to Iraq.

HONDROS: See? Can you imagine?

AMOS: I just want to say about the good news—I've said this many times so if anyone has heard me do it, I'm sorry. Somehow we allowed, as journalists, I think, we let the CPA, the White House, and the entire establishment in Washington get away with defining news as good or bad.

And no one stood up and said, "But that's not what we do. We don't do the good news. We do the news." Because we were outside the Green Zone we were seeing a different Iraq than those officials were. And I never saw even our bosses stand up and challenge that language. It stands to this day. I'm sure that you know you can have this argument with soldiers, and I have when I've spoken in military classrooms, where

they still challenge me and say, "Why didn't you do the good news?" And I do make this argument: "Not my job!"

HONDROS: It's part of the same thing. Just like most people who haven't been to war zones imagine a war zone is twenty-four hours a day, fighting every square inch of the country, moment you get off the plane someone shoots at you. Which of course is not the case. And anybody with war-zone experience knows that even in the most brutal destroyed countries street level commerce often continues.

People live their lives. In the worst, worst days of the South Bronx, street life was vibrant. It didn't make it a good place to be or mean it didn't need some help but…so I think it's the same kind of thing. They say, "Where are the good news stories?" When they go on their patrols they see shops open, they see people running around. They're not experienced. And they think well, this must be pretty good. "The Iraqis look pretty happy to me. They're running around, They're laughing on the sidewalks and things like that."

CHANDRASEKARAN: I think one of the most telling stories that we did at the *Post* was done as a double bylined effort by my very intrepid, incredibly talented Arabic-speaking colleague, Anthony Shadid, who won the 2004 Pulitzer for international reporting, and our incredibly brilliant military correspondent, Tom Ricks, who's written the best-selling book *Fiasco*. The two of them went on a military patrol. I think this was in late 2003. And Tom was with the soldiers and going with them from house to house and shop to shop. There'd be this guy saying, "Hey, I'm the new boss in town," and Achmad shaking his hand. "Made a new friend there. We got them on our side."

Anthony would sidle up about five minutes later and talk to the same guy. "Those Americans. They're out here. I'm sure they're going to come back and rape my daughter." There was just this mistrust. In some cases they would say one thing to the Americans and say another thing when they weren't talking to the American soldiers. In other cases it was just an interpretation that these soldiers had. Yes, they were being greeted warmly and this person was on our side. When in fact, that just wasn't the case.

HONDROS: It's that same naïveté. Just because they sit down and have tea with you—everybody would say that, "Oh we sit and have tea with the people all the time." Well, that doesn't mean anything.

CHANDRASEKARAN: They'll have tea with anybody.

HONDROS: Exactly. That doesn't mean anything.

FADHIL: I just want to mention that I disagree with argument that westerners did not report the good news. I remember at NPR we were reporting how the Iraqis started buying satellite dishes. They are now free to see…I mean these were the good news stories in the beginning. The cell phones, all this stuff. How we were able for the first time to see the European porno channels through the satellite [laughter]. Stuff like that. That didn't last long. We were doing this in 2004. Most of 2004, we were also reporting about how Iraqis were now free to have their own organizations. For example, women things. A lot of good things. It's just that the bad news, if you compare it to the good news, we have a lot of bad news in Iraq. That's a problem.

HONDROS: They set the bar too high anyway. Also the good news was supposed to be to create this Jeffersonian peaceful democracy in Iraq that would lead the region. That was the bar that they set themselves. When the bar is so high and it isn't reached anywhere near that, of course, the perspective…

AMOS: But you don't hear much of that anymore, that idea that somehow…

HONDROS: You still kind of do. An Iraq that defends and no… what does [President Bush] say, "A peaceful secure Iraq that is peaceful with its neighbor, that is able to defend and secure itself"…something like that.

GRAHAM: It's related to the idea of good guy [versus] bad guy. It's the same mentality.

As soon as you heard someone say "bad guy" you thought, "Oh my God," especially because in Iraq the bad guys were the Americans almost universally. Even if people were happy that Saddam was gone there was a great deal of resentment against the occupation.

AMOS: Well, there was a time in Baghdad where the CPA Web site had a meter that showed how much electricity they could give to Baghdad. The problem was the insurgency used it as a marker, so every time they blew something up the marker would go this way. I'm not making this up. So the CPA had to take it off the Web site so that there couldn't be a measure between who was winning and losing between the CPA and the insurgency.

CHANDRASEKARAN: And you've got to remember, each of these "Oh well, we've made great progress with electricity"— the initial American promise as stated by Ambassador Bremer repeatedly, again and again, was that they would be producing 6,000 megawatts of electricity by the summer of 2004. They're not even doing that. They're barely doing what they did under Saddam, and that was under UN sanctions. Each one of these things has to be looked at in the boarder context of what the initial promise, the pledge, was.

CJR: What Patrick said earlier was that the truth and the facts aren't that close in this instant. I'm wondering what the panelists

think about that.

AMOS: As time went on, we had our paradise but slowly over time the window of what we can see in Iraq has closed. However, that is never reflected in any of our copy. We never say, "And now we hired some guards, and now we can't go out without a full abayah, and now we can't go out at all. Now everything we do is through our Iraqi staff because it's too dangerous for us to go out."

So when you pick up your newspapers or turn on your radio, it looks normal. It looks like it looked in 2003. The copy is still there, the sound is still there, you can't tell the difference. But we know that our jobs and the way we do them are so constricted, but there is no little warning at the end that you're not getting the full details here.

I think everybody did that. Every journalist in Iraq did that. From 2003 until today without having a health risk warning at the top of the copy.

It's true that [Farnaz Fassihi's e-mail in September 2004] was personal and so people got it, but I think the shock of that e-mail was because we haven't fessed up as a group. That you just aren't getting the story anymore, not the way you were.

GRAHAM: I think it's just limitations of journalists. The United States is such an all-consuming culture and its view of itself, its sort of self-regard, is so powerful, this sort of Heisenberg thing, it kind of influences everything.

Europeans I don't think have any problem with it. And the Brits didn't. I wrote for *The Observer*, and you could write anything for *The Observer*. And it's not because they have a looser relationship with facts, as the Americans say. They kind of trust you.

The notion of verifiable fact in journalism to some extent was a stumbling block against what had to be was interpretation. And a lot of American interpreters or people like Christopher Hitchens or Thomas Friedman, influential people, who flew in and did not know what they were talking about and wrote stuff that was just nonsense and still do. There goes my career [laughter]. The interpretations of what's happening—I spent so much time fact-checking. You can't do that in a place like Iraq. You just can't. It just was impossible in the end.

Ali must have found it almost strange to arrive in a world where everything had to be fact-checked because you think, "Well, I know that."

FADHIL: It's not only this. It's because I know there is no way to fact check what you can. Right now when I read stories in *The New York Times*, to be honest I find it's more close to reality than before. And the reason why, I think…

GRAHAM: Because the journalists can't go out.

FADHIL: Exactly. It's coming through the Iraqis who are working with them, who know the place. I mean I'm pro-Iraqi [laughter]. Seriously, the stories I'm reading right now are more close to what's happening exactly. Sometimes I wonder how they got this. Even Iraqis cannot get this fact. I mean they cannot get this. It's kind of different from what it was two years ago. I don't know how you perceive it. You perceive it in a way, for you this is nonsense. [To Graham:] You're Canadian, we cannot trust you.

Seriously, I believe that because it is going through the Iraqis and they are depending on the Iraqis more, it is becoming close to what is happening really on the ground. Is it fair? I don't know. Is it like everything is fact checked? I don't know. But I doubt you can do fact-checking for what's coming in the news today. You should just buy it because it is very difficult. What they are getting is good. It's amazing for me as an Iraqi. I read it here, I read it in the way they are putting it. I believe it, but again it's very difficult to verify.

CJR: Let me now turn this open to questions.

QUESTION: My question is about the book *Lapdogs* [by Eric Boehlert], the thesis of which, as I understand it, is a critique of the media for having allowed the White House and presumably also the Coalition [Provisional] Authority to get by on a whole range of issues, and it seems that you folks are not part of that critique. So is it your editors back in the states who let the play, the framing, the understanding of the war always slide to a Bush-administration-sympathetic position, or was it the other journalists, or was it just certain journalists with a particular ideological axe to grind? It would seem that *Lapdogs* makes a pretty comprehensive and thorough critique. What do you think?

HONDROS: Well, you hear that a lot but I think journalists have had very little to do with it in Iraq from the very beginning. The invasion of Iraq was going to go on no matter what journalists did, and the way Iraq is ending up right now, if no western journalists had set foot in Iraq, I don't know that Iraq would look much different right now than it does.

It's important that the American people have been kept, to some degree, informed but I don't know that we've been so decisive in the conduct of this war. In fact, I've been kind of amazed by how little impact, generally speaking, we've had.

No one knows what might have happened in alternate plays of reality and fate. But my impression is that journalism isn't perfect and there was a lot of credibility given to wrong ideas in the run up to the war. I don't know that it was a decisive factor in the fact that the war went down. I think it was going to go down either way. That's my personal opinion.

CHANDRASEKARAN: Just briefly. If we take the period from April 2003 on, and I don't want to sound defensive here, but I would put the coverage that appeared in *The Washington Post* up for any sort of scrutiny anybody would want to offer. I haven't read the book *Lapdogs* but if you go back and you look at the dispatches that were coming out of our bureau there, there were clearly lengthy stories, we're talking 3,000-word stories on several occasions talking about the growth of Moqtada al-Sadr and tensions within the Shiite community, the growth of the Sunni-led insurgency, problems with the Coalition Provisional Authority, the military's inability to hold places in the country. Questions about troop strength.

I think it was there in a number of publications. Because I was fairly busy over there I didn't have a chance to watch a lot of domestic television coverage, and I think that is a subject that probably is deserving of a little bit more scrutiny and criticism. I'd like to think that at least the work we did out there, I'd be more than happy to put it up to any sort of test or criticism. I think that there was a lot of very, very critical on-the-ground reporting that was done by a number of very brave journalists from the very beginning.

QUESTION: Two quick questions. One for Ms. Amos. Why isn't coverage of the coverage more obvious in the news media? Two, to Rajiv, you're now a news administrator as an assistant managing editor. Why aren't stories from embedded reporters labeled as such, and why aren't the conditions under which these people operate given to the readers?

AMOS: I personally think it is because, as I said, that Iraq is a singular kind of place. Over these years, the coverage and the ways that we go about our coverage have forced us to be creative. And no one has actually asked the question of should we tell our listeners how we do this now? We don't talk about it in the newsroom, we really don't. I mean it took us a while even to give the Iraqis, who are our journalists, bylines. The print people were doing it a whole lot faster than we were. The television people don't do it at all. I suppose it's awkward. Where do you put it in a television report?

I think the media has not dealt with this issue about how we do things. Every once in a while you'll see, it was either John Burns or Dexter Filkins say it takes five times as long to get a story in Iraq as it does anyplace else on the planet. You'll see little sparks of it, but there's been no writing about and no talking about it.

CHANDRASEKARAN: What Deb was saying, I think that we could all stand to do a little bit more coverage of how we all operate there. I've got to say, a piece I did for the *Post* Outlook section about operating as a journalist in Baghdad probably elicited more e-mails than any other single story that I wrote while I was there, including a 5,000-word piece I did about the failings of the CPA.

But to your point about embedding: I don't think it's all that necessary and let me explain why. I think that during the war it is

eminently clear when dispatches are coming from embedded journalists. You're with a certain unit. I think that's fairly transparent to the reader or the television viewer.

I think that today, when you look at the stories that are done by journalists who are embedded with military units, it's so clear that they are with them, and in many cases, I think, when I look at print journalism, the stories that have been done by my colleagues at the *Post* and people at *The New York Times*, from embedded capacity, I think they've actually been incredibly critical of many of the high-level strategic decisions that have been made by the U.S. military.

I point to the series of stories written by Steve Fainaru [of *The Washington Post*], who was a finalist for the Pulitzer international reporting last year, all done in an embedded capacity, and I don't think you could look at any of them and say this guy was duped or that he was simply giving one side of the story. You have to accept it for what it is. A story written by a journalist who is embedded with soldiers up in Mosul is not a story that tells you exactly what is happening up in Mosul, or it shouldn't be. And news organizations shouldn't delude themselves into thinking it is. You clearly don't get that perspective but you do get what I think is an incredibly valuable perspective into sort of things like a window into the life of the grunt.

QUESTION: But wouldn't it help a reader to know that this reporter is operating under conditions where he is restricted in being able to quote the people he is with?

CHANDRASEKARAN: If, in fact, that is the case. In my experiences with being embedded, I haven't often run up against situations where people have been unwilling to be quoted, at least no more so than when reporting in the Republican Palace or in any other part of the federal bureaucracy.

QUESTION: My understanding is that you sign a document saying you won't do it.

HONDROS: You sign a document saying you won't show—the major thrust of the document is that you won't give away operational security, which is basically like they're going to invade somebody in the next day and you don't say it.

CHANDRASEKARAN: Just speaking for myself, I have never felt that I had to hold back on anything as an embedded reporter other than something like, the marines I'm with are going to be moving into this part of Fallujah tomorrow. Not disclosing anything operational. I have not felt that. Others may have felt that but just speaking personally I have not.

QUESTION: This is a question for Ali. We haven't really talked about this. You wrote in *The New York Times* about being part of this first generation of free Iraqi journalists, and it has been my experience working with you and working with other Iraqi journalists, compared to working with other parts of the world like Syria where I train journalists, that Iraqi journalists have been so much more energized and able to engage in critical thinking and take initiative and embrace the profession as western journalists have defined it, and I just thought perhaps it might be interesting to people to ask you what happened there? What created this sudden outpouring and curiosity and energy?

FADHIL: I think it was the years we lived under Saddam's regime. We had this kind of journalism that talks in the mouth of the regime, Saddam himself. And when the invasion happened, although we were against it, you find many of the journalists—Sunni, Shiite, whatever—they are against it, against the invasion, against the war because they knew people who died, at least most of them.

But the war sort of created for us this new vision to how the world is. The media for us, as Iraqis working with western journalists, was like a new world. Sitting with western journalists learning from them, working with Andrew, working with Patrick, with Anne Garrels, George Packer, others, it's like a kind of training. It's live training on the ground. You go with them, you're a translator you get this from them. You see how they start questions and then end up with a question that resembles the first question in a way. You see the technique and think, "Okay, that's a new thing. I didn't know that journalism can do that." It's even useful for medicine. You can get people to say things, for example, about STDs.

This sort of new era of looking at your country in a new angle—you become not just Iraqi but you become an international Iraqi. You look at the people from a different lens. That created the curiosity inside me and for some friends I know, besides we really want to get in to this profession. We really want to be good at it.

GRAHAM: Also, there were just really good Iraqi journalists. Ali is superb. And Ghaith Abdul-Ahad had stuff in *The Guardian*—there's just not a journalist working anywhere, there's nobody as good as Ghaith. Was it during the elections? He went out with an insurgent leader, with the guy stuffing ballot boxes. Stuff that as a westerner you couldn't imagine getting and just written like he understood the language, which is something else we haven't really touched on too much. This incredible language barrier, and which is why *The Washington Post* stuff with Anthony was just like head and shoulders above the rest. And that was Anthony. No, Rajiv too. But Anthony was amazing to watch, how he understood particularly the Shia, his enormous sympathy, and one of the great things about Iraq is this production of these really talented, bright, bilingual people.

CHANDRASEKARAN: But even Anthony had some limitations in that after a while they

knew he wasn't an Iraqi, he was of Lebanese descent. Nobody can get the same access in Iraq as an Iraqi.

FADHIL: But that was before. Right now even if you're Iraqi, you're a journalist and that means something really bad.

CHANDRASEKARAN: Even though you're an Iraqi, you can't go and hang out in Fallujah for three weeks on your own.

FADHIL: No way, no way. Even in Baghdad. If you talk to people—you cannot stay in the place in a street for more than an hour, even if you're an Iraqi, because it's dangerous. They might be insurgents, they might be informants for insurgents on the street. Just call them and they can come by on motorcycle and just shoot you that easily. Because you're a journalist, you can be killed. That's the only reason.

It's for two things. First because a journalist in Iraq means you're allied with either the Americans, the Iraq government, or westerners in general. Or the second thing, in Islam, in extreme Islam, not Islam as a religion, but in extremist Islam, journalism is something regarded as forbidden, *haram*, for many reasons, for ridiculous reasons you don't want to hear it, actually.

GRAHAM: Journalism was revolutionized in Iraq by an Iraqi—when Salam Pax did his blogging. You know, during the war that was the most extraordinary kind of journalism. No war will ever be covered the same because of Salam Pax.

AMOS: And he actually revolutionized blogging in the Arab world because the Jordanians took off after that, the Syrians. He really opened up something quite remarkable.

GRAHAM: And it's very Iraqi too. That intimacy. It's such an intimate culture where it was about his family. When you spend time in Iraq, that is so much of how you spend time with people. It was an expression of this, talking about personal point of view, it was just more intimate than a westerner would have been during the war. It was incredible.

FADHIL: It's really the presence of westerners in Baghdad that drove us to this kind of journalism, to go to pursue the career of journalism and the media. It's really the presence of westerners in Iraq. For me that was the motive. I see them in places, in rural places in Iraq. I would never think of going to these places, and they go just for the sake of the story. And that's for me something, a very big thing for me actually. I thought these people are crazy enough to do these things. I want to be crazy like that.

QUESTION: Mr. Hondros, you mentioned when you go out and do your work, you're wondering will anyone back home see

this, will anyone even care? I think that's important. What made me really start to care was a photo essay of Iraq girls, fifteen- and sixteen-year-olds locked in their bedrooms, and this was their adolescence—an age we celebrate here, and they were spending it not being able to do anything. I'm wondering for you, and for all of you, when you go out, how much do you think about this? How will I make them care? How do I cover something that is going to make them care?

HONDROS: Well, anytime you do any journalism you want to do it in a way that has impact. The thing about it to me, and I've seen this especially in Iraq, is what makes people care—we care about different things, even as Americans. So a little girl whose parents just got shot, and now she's orphaned by U.S. soldiers. To some people that is just proof positive, they don't need any more proof that this is a bad war, a bad thing. Forget it. To some people, well, that's war and that's what happens in war and we're bringing something noble to the people, these kinds of things are going to happen and there is a larger positive thing. Same set of facts, same set of circumstances, and I think that's a reason why some of our journalism hasn't had the monolithic impact or something, sometimes, because everybody takes from it different things, what they want to see. All you can do is just go there, be true to your personal journalistic ideals, and do work of the best quality you can, and hope that there is some good in the universe.

QUESTION: I sense that one of the things that is going on for you is a sense of catharsis. You've obviously faced some difficult situations and now you're here to express them to a larger audience. As a former marine public affairs officer, it is interesting to see this side of it. My question is more of a policy one. I am a student at the School of International Public Affairs [at Columbia University]. And it's just a real cliché basic question: What the hell should we do now? You are policy experts.

HONDROS: Nobody asked us up to this point, why should they listen to us now? Seriously, any journalist by April 2004, or as Rajiv was saying, the summer of 2004, I think every journalist knew that what we are in now, two-and-a-half years later, was going to come. This pie-in-the-sky vision was hopeless. And this thing is pretty much going to fall apart. The basics on the ground had no possibility of keeping this thing together. And now, two-and-a-half years later, what was apparent to most journalists is getting to be apparent to the American people. So, why should anybody listen to us now? We already knew that way back in the day. So what we do from here? I have my personal opinions, but I'm not sure anyone is interested in them, really.

FADHIL: I think this way. I'm a doctor. I'm twenty-seven in 2003. I arrived in June

2003, after the invasion. In August [2003] things were getting worse and I knew Iraq was going to hell. And that's why I changed from one thing to another thing. But I'm just a physician, I don't know anything about policy. I would describe myself as a kid at that time. Right now, I know a lot because of the media, but at that time I knew nothing about Iraq. And I knew things were going to be worse. Not only me, a guy who sells fruits in Sadr City knew things were going to hell. Things were going downwards. Everyone knew that. We were saying, Patrick remembers, anyone asks us, we said now things are going bad because they are giving the leadership to the wrong people, people who don't know the Iraqis. Whatever. That's our simple interpretation as Iraqis. Now, you, the government, the think tanks of the United States, you don't know things were going worse? I mean, for me, that's amazing! If we, as simple Iraqis, can tell, how can you Americans who came into Iraq with 180,000 troops, you don't know things were going bad in Iraq? That's ridiculous!

CHANDRASEKARAN: As a working journalist, I am going to shy away from prescribing policy but I will, however, say that in my continued discussion with people both in and out of government and in and out of Iraq, clearly I haven't stumbled upon anybody yet who has sort of a magic bullet scenario. Look, it's obvious to all of us that the current strategy has led to one hundred plus American service members dying last month and hundreds upon hundreds of Iraqis dying and many more wounded. But if American troops were to leave there are a lot of smart people who say that the daily toll from the sectarian violence would go from the many dozens to the many hundreds. And is that something people would find morally acceptable?

There are other smart people who say that if you were to try and partition the country up and force large or at least encourage large groups of the population to move from one place to another you could wind up sparking the broader civil strife— the broader civil war that you are trying to prevent from this.

It seems that every good option on the table is fraught with peril. I suppose the one noncontroversial thing I could say is it is my sincere hope as an individual, and even as a journalist, that at the very least this country could engage in an honest non-partisan discussion in Washington about the way forward. Unfortunately, Iraq policy has become so politicized that national discussion and the discussion inside Washington that is required to come up with a workable scenario that is in the best interest of the Iraqi people and in the best interest of the United States is still elusive.

GRAHAM: Your question is a very American question. Your question suggests that there is a solution. I don't know why Americans think there is a solution. Why should there be a solution? As Ali says, Iraqis have been

saying almost since the statue fell that there were serious problems. And they were told by journalists and by everybody that they were basically whining.

I came back in August 2003 and I was sat down by a friend of mine—a very important businessman, and he said, "This country is going to hell. The Sufis and the Salafis are getting together to fight the Americans."

You couldn't have found an editor in the States who would have published a story about the relationship between Sufis and the Salafis, but it was fundamental to Iraq. Why do people—I understand it's a very marine question, but why do people think there is a solution? There isn't. That's its tragedy.

QUESTION: You've all spoken to one degree or another about the misunderstandings of our troops, be they misunderstandings of culture or misunderstandings of the relationship between them and Iraqi civilians, and it's been getting a little better lately, but certainly at the beginning I didn't see a lot of coverage or enough coverage on that. I wonder if you feel that it was because reporters in general are worried that any negative comment would label them as unsupportive of our troops, and if that's true how you get around that?

AMOS: There was a fair amount of coverage about that in the beginning, about people who didn't speak any Arabic. Remember, early on that one of Fallujah's complaints was about sunglasses. That they felt

Americans were looking up the skirts of Iraqi women in the most conservative town in the country. And if that didn't scream cultural problem, I don't know what did.

QUESTION: I'm struck by this idea of Iraqi journalists who are being trained as a parallel, and that's a largely uncovered story as opposed to the well-covered story of the Iraqi security forces who are being trained. While the journalists seem to be going out and being unsung doing their job and taking over these roles from American journalists who are unable to work in the field anymore, the security forces are failing to a large extent. My question is, for western journalists, you talked about coming from this utopia for journalists where you could go out and work and talk to anyone and now having that window shut off for you, and I'm wondering about how you went through that process of turning it over to people who, as Ali says, can actually report a lot of the stories better. And at the same time, while it's now too unsafe for western journalists to go out, that doesn't mean it is safe for Iraqi journalists to go out. So what sort of responsibilities do you feel toward them as their taking over this role in the western press?

FADHIL: It is dangerous for us, yes. It is getting more dangerous for us, yes. As I said, the reason why we are doing this is because—I don't want to call it country-driven or people-driven because I don't want to sound biased in our coverage. Many of us are coming from different ethnicities, some are Shia, some are Sunnis covering each side and doing it fairly enough.

But we still have, we still feel inside ourselves a responsibility to the Iraqi people that we should tell the people what is going on inside. This is what's going on. People have to know what's happening in this place, what's happening in that place. It's a kind of commitment to our own people. I would say it that way.

AMOS: I will just say it is a horrible responsibility. We worry about them all the time because the relationship you have with your interpreter, translator, whatever you want to call them, is the most intimate relationship I can think of that has nothing to do with sex. You are in a mind meld; you have to trust each other, you are out together. They see things that you can't possibly see, and you have to have an intellectual relationship with them that is remarkable. And when you've done that for a while day after day after day, of course you worry about them, you worry about them like you worry about your children. You know that because they worked with you they want to go out there and do the things that we did. We just can't go anymore. It's a very emotional relationship to think about them out there.

CHANDRASEKARAN: They are the true

heroes of the press corps. Make no mistake about it. These are people who put their lives on the line every single day. Okay, every foreign journalist is under some degree of threat but our Iraqi staffers are under threat the moment well, they're under threat when they're sleeping and they're at home. We've had people who have had bad guys banging on the door looking for them. They're followed to work in some cases. The amount of stress and danger that they deal with on any given day is out of this world. And they have my everlasting respect.

You know, I would love to see a television documentary or a front-page story that writes about their lives, but again, that would put them in a degree of risk and danger that you don't want to. We like to give them bylines as much as possible, but there are cases where we can't put their names in the paper and that's for their own safety.

HONDROS: And they have died. We've lost many, many good friends. A number of Iraqi journalists allied with western media.

GRAHAM: Particularly cameramen

HONDROS: Cameramen and others too.

QUESTION: As a journalism student here who is very interested in covering conflict, I was wondering if you could give me last-minute advice on something you would have done differently or something you wish people had told you before you got into this, and maybe if it's possible to speak specifically to how you negotiate not becoming desensitized yet not emotionally overwhelmed as well.

HONDROS: We may have to free up an extra hour if we're going to talk about that.

CHANDRASEKARAN: I'll make it quick. As an aspiring journalist, DON'T go to Iraq. I mean that in all seriousness. If you're a freelancer and you're not working for a major news organization, you don't have all the requisite resources in terms of security, insurance, all of that other stuff. If you haven't covered other conflicts in other places, don't just try to parachute into Iraq. It is the most dangerous thing you could possibly do.

FADHIL: Especially the kidnapping insurance.

GRAHAM: I think most people get their start by going somewhere, and if you're lucky the American government will spend $350 billion after you get there. Maybe go to Tehran.

Acknowledgments

Late in 2006 one of our contributing editors, Michael Massing, had an idea for *Columbia Journalism Review*. The magazine, he suggested, should interview reporters covering the war in Iraq and, out of their collected insights and anecdotes, create an oral history. We jumped at the idea. For one thing, the character of the war and the daily lives of millions of Iraqis had changed drastically since the March 2003 invasion. Who knew more about the chemistry of those changes than the journalists who reported on them? For another, the journalists' working conditions had changed utterly. During the first year of the occupation, reporters, photographers, and producers roamed the country freely, talking to Iraqis with ease; three years later they were in grave danger almost anywhere in Iraq, and employing creative and courageous ways to do their work.

The journalists were eager to talk, and they provided us with wisdom and stories enough for an article-length oral history and, one year later, this book. We want to thank Massing for the idea and the advice he provided along the way. We'd also like to thank the Open Society Institute, whose generous support and encouragement made this project possible.

We are particularly grateful to our three main interviewers: Vivienne Walt, Christopher Allbritton, and Judith Matloff. Walt is a seasoned correspondent for *Newsweek* and other outlets who herself has come under fire more than once in Iraq; Allbritton moved to Iraq shortly before the war and set himself up as a stringer and an innovative reader-supported blogger. Matloff has covered conflicts for some twenty years in Africa and elsewhere.

We'd also like to thank Nancy Novick, our photo editor, for her thorough research and sharp visual sense. Nancy pored over thousands of photographs in search of the visual dimensions of this history. We'd like to thank Bruce Wallace for his assiduous and acute editorial assistance during the transformation of the oral history into a book. Also our interview transcribers: Emma Hoyt, Timothy K. Hoyt, Lucia Graves, Lawrence Lanahan, Georgia Schoonmaker, Ezra Selove, and Eliza Shapiro.

Most of all, we would like express our profound gratitude to the forty-six reporters, photographers, and editors who so generously gave us their time and their insights about the coverage of this long, hard war.

Mike Hoyt
John Palattella

Columbia Journalism Review's mission is to encourage and stimulate excellence in journalism in the service of a free society. Founded in 1961 under the auspices of Columbia University's Graduate School of Journalism, CJR examines day-to-day press performance as well as the forces that affect that performance. The magazine is published six times a year, and offers a deliberative mix of reporting, analysis, criticism, and commentary. CJR.org, our Web site, delivers real-time criticism and reporting, giving CJR a vital presence in the ongoing conversation about the media. Both online and in print, *Columbia Journalism Review* is in conversation with a community of people who share a commitment to high journalistic standards in the U.S. and the world.

To subscribe to *Columbia Journalism Review* call 888-425-7782, or mail $27.95 for one year, $41.95 for two years, to:

CJR
P.O. BOX 578
MT. MORRIS, ILLINOIS
61054

Or subscribe through the Web site at www.cjr.org

About the Editors

MIKE HOYT is the executive editor of *Columbia Journalism Review*, both the bimonthly magazine and the daily CJR.org. He has worked as a writer and editor at the magazine since 1986. Before that he was a freelance magazine writer, a copy editor for *Business Week*, and a reporter at two New Jersey dailies, *The Record*, in Bergen County, and *The Home News*, then in New Brunswick. He grew up in Kansas City, Missouri, and lives in New Jersey with his wife, Mary Ellen Schoonmaker.

JOHN PALATTELLA is the literary editor of *The Nation* and a former editor at large of the *Columbia Journalism Review* and a former special projects editor at *Lingua Franca*. He was born in Port Washington, New York, and grew up in New York, Ohio, and Connecticut. His essays and reviews have appeared in numerous publications, including *The Nation*, the *London Review of Books, Boston Review, Bookforum*, the *Los Angeles Times Book Review*, and *The Washington Post Bookworld*.